CHALLENGE ACCEPTED!

CHALLENGE ACCEPTED!

253 STEPS TO BECOMING AN ANTI–IT GIRL

CELESTE BARBER

amazon publishing

Published by Amazon Publishing, Seattle

www.apub.com

Amazon, the Amazon logo, and Amazon Publishing are trademarks of Amazon.com,
Inc., or its affiliates.

First published in 2018 by HarperCollins*Publishers* Australia Pty Limited

ISBN-13: 9781542006231 (hardcover)
ISBN-10: 1542006236 (hardcover)
ISBN-13: 9781542006248 (paperback)
ISBN-10: 1542006244 (paperback)

Cover Design by Mark Campbell, HarperCollins Design Studio

Cover Photography by Corrine Bond, Vivien's Creative

Printed in the United States of America

First edition

For JoJo, Mark, and Nic.
Come back now please, I've got so much to tell you.

The One with All the Content

Dear America   1

Pilot   5

The One
    . . . Where I Thought I Would Flip Inside Out   9
    . . . Where I Discovered Ritalin, My Childhood (Not So)
        Imaginary Friend   21
    . . . About My Dad   35
    . . . Where I Danced a Lot   41
    . . . About My #metoo Stories (Sad Face Emoji)   47
    . . . About My Fake Brother, Michael   55
    . . . Where I Was Bullied at School, I Think   61
    . . . About Falling in Love with Comedy   75
    . . . About Surviving Drama School   83
    . . . With Another Gross Man #timesup   89
    . . . About Sparky   99
    . . . About Thomas   107
    . . . About My Love for the LGBTQI Community   113
    . . . With #hothusband   117

Dear Wine   135

The One
    . . . Where My Heart Was Cut Open   137
    . . . About My Breasts   155

Dear Hangover   159

The One

. . . About My Mum   161
. . . About Jo and How I Got in Trouble at Yoga   167
. . . Where I Discover Being Famous on Instagram
      Is Like Being Rich at Monopoly   175
. . . Where I Go to America   183
. . . When Harry Met Celeste   193
. . . Where I Become an #accidental(role)model   201
. . . About Loving Our Bodies #bopo   211
. . . With My 28-Day Journey to Better Diet and Exercise   215
. . . Where I Explain Why I Don't Hate Hot People   223
. . . No One Cares About   227
. . . Where I Became an Anti-Influencer   231

The Last One Part 1 (Celisticles)   239

The Last One Part 2 (Acknowledgments)   243

Dear Parents   245

About the Author   247

Dear America

How are y'all?

I'm that crazy Australian who takes photos of herself. That lady who tries to make you laugh and show that we shouldn't take ourselves too seriously. You know her? Yep, that's me!

I wanted to take this opportunity (that was 100 percent forced on me by my US publisher) to write an additional introduction ahead of the standard introduction I had already written to thank y'all personally for being so super supportive of me and all my shenanigans and for allowing me to penetrate you just the right amount.

You are the most supportive of all the lands, and it's a really nice feeling, because you own some of the things that I hold closest to my heart . . .

Malt milkshakes.

Queer Eye for the Straight Guy—the original AND the reboot.

An entire channel dedicated to BRAVO!

And TOM MUTHAFUCKING FORD.

I was recently in you for New York Fashion Week, obvs, and I'm not going to lie to you—it was a bag of mixed nuts. Some were shitty Brazilian-type nuts, like when I was asked on two separate occasions by two European supermodels when shopping in Bloomingdale's to fetch them a different size in jeans, and when I told them I didn't work there, they were already bored of my "attitude" and had moved on to another mother of two who was trying to have a quick five minutes to herself.

But I also had some really yummy chocolate-coated hazelnut-type experiences. I met everyone's favorite uncle, Tom Hanks, got to make out with everyone's wet dream, Tom Ford, and witnessed Serena Williams continue her quest to dismantle the patriarchy—in a tutu!

Since I'm going to be hanging out with you guys a lot more, I needed to get my Social Security card so I can work and not be stopped at the border and have my children ripped from me because I'm trying to do the best I can. When I told the man at the Social Security office that I was there for Fashion Week, he responded, "Oh, so you're a photographer?" When I looked at him blankly, he corrected himself by saying, "Manager?" To which I responded, "Why don't you assume I'm a model?" With that he stamped my Social Security passport-type card thingy and, avoiding any direct eye contact, sent me on my way with a handful of sympathy candy.

After this last trip (the one where I made out with Tom Ford; have I mentioned that?), there is one lingering question I have and was hoping you might be able to shed some light on . . .

What's with listing all the side effects in your ads for pharmaceutical drugs? Never have I heard the words "renal bleeding" alongside "infant formula" more in my life than when I spent half an hour watching TV in my overpriced East Village Airbnb. DM me.

There are a few things that us Aussies do really well that you guys need to get across:

Fairy bread—white bread with butter and sprinkles, that's it. Fairy bread.

Beaches—we are so goddamned good at beaches, you guys, it's kind of crazy.

Slang—our slang is like nothing else. Let me give you an example.

Man in any country in the world other than Australia talking to friend:

"Before I head off I want you to know that the guy over there looks exactly like your ex. I think he's interested in you and wants to go on a date. Here, I got you a coffee."

Man in Australia, most likely Queensland, talking to friend:

"Before I hit the frog and toad, you should know that that rooster is a dead ringer for your mate, and I'm pretty sure he's as keen as mustard and is gagging to have a crack. Here, wrap your laughing gear around this."

You guys and gals have the ability to make me feel as though I'm better than I really am, and I fucking love it. We're not so hot at this in the wonderful land of Oz; what we *do* do, however, is produce not one, not two, but three incredible-looking men that are all related and go by the name of Hemsworth.

So thanks for the former, and you're welcome for the latter.

Big love,

Celeste

P.S. Slipping off the chair at the end of the Tom Ford make-out video—wasn't acting.

Pilot

Well hello, you cheeky little saucepots. Thank you for buying my book (or thank you for acting excited when it was given to you by your sister-in-law, who probably bought it last minute while running through the airport trying not to miss family Christmas).

I bet you're thinking, "She's just like me!"—except when you saw the cover and probably realized that I've completely got my head up my own arse. And I know for sure that my primary school tutor—let's just call her Mrs. Fleet—is thinking, "Oh my God, if this chick can get a book deal, then anything is possible." And you're right, Mrs. Fleet. Anything is possible, even though you treated me like I was illiterate when we all knew I was dyslexic with ADD.

This book is a massive deal for me, not only because the profits will help keep my gray hair under control, but because y'all have been super kind and supportive of me and my stuff, and buying this book is a part of that. (No, you shut up; *you're* getting emotional in the intro.)

The closest I ever got to writing a book was at primary school, when most recesses and lunchtimes were spent writing lines: "I will not talk back to the teacher. I will not talk back to the teacher." And I filled up those pages pretty quickly. So I'm hoping this will be pretty similar.

I love writing. Even though I'm no wordsmith, I spell and read words phonetically, and autocorrect can't fix or find replacements for 98 percent of what I write. I've always enjoyed expressing myself with a pen and paper. That was until I started writing this book, and now I'm so fucking stressed that I want to go and scream into a pillow. But how good is the cover, right?!

Now, for those of you thinking, "Oh God, I just spent *actual* money on a book by a girl who is only good at taking inappropriate unflattering photos of herself"—never fear! I'm going to tackle a lot of big issues in this book, from how rich Bill Gates really is to why laser hair removal is more effective on dark hair than on fair hair.[1] Here are five reasons why buying this book was a good idea:

1. You went into a bookshop to get it—yay! Everyone wants to fuck someone who pretends to be smart. Or if you got it online, you can just click straight back over to Pornhub[2] after purchasing it and get your fix there—whatever blows your hair back.

2. If you hate it, you can totally regift it to a middle-aged woman named Beverly—they seem to think I'm pretty cool.

---

1   That's a lie. I don't discuss Bill Gates or hair removal once in this book; I was lying to make you laugh. Please get used to it, because I do it a fair bit in the pages that follow. I have a real desire to make people laugh, no matter what the cost. I'm seeing someone about it.

2   This book has in no way been funded by Pornhub, nor do the nice people at Amazon Publishing have any affiliation with Pornhub (to my knowledge). It was just a joke. A joke that I'm now having to explain. And we all know, those are the best kind. And here's a neat drinking game, which you can play while you're reading. Every time you read the word "emoji" you need to drink. This is also the case for the words "and," "the," "#hothusband," and "cervix." CUT LOOSE.

3. By purchasing this book, you have helped me buy school shoes for my kids. They say thank you for that.

4. People will think you're a feminist, and everyone *loves* a feminist. Just ask Germaine Greer.

5. If Brandi Glanville (google her, she'll love it) can write a *New York Times* bestseller, then so can I.

The One Where I Thought I Would Flip Inside Out

I've never really known how people start books, especially memoirs. And especially not one by someone who is thirty-six, which is kind of weird considering I haven't even started my second and chosen career as the new and slightly less busty Michelle Visage. So I thought I'd just jump straight in with one of my favorite stories. Here it is, the story about the day I met my first son and how my once-neat vagina became one big hole.

Does anyone really plan pregnancies? I mean seriously? In my experience, they have been a bloody big surprise, and not the delivery-guy-turned-up-with-something-you-forgot-you-bought-online-weeks-earlier kind of surprise, but more of a "sorry we are out of bacon today" kind of surprise at your local café. It's unnerving at the beginning, but you know it's the best thing for you in the long run.

I have four kids. I have two boys of my very own who came tearing out of me, and I inherited two girls—a package deal with my husband, Api. Sahra was two and Kyah was four when I first met them. I have been a stepmother since the age of twenty-one.

I had my first boy in a small town on the Mid North Coast of New South Wales. Api had bought a house there after his first daughter was born, and when I found out I was pregnant, I moved up there with him. For those of you playing at home, who have no idea where the hell I'm talking about, the Mid North Coast is an area on the east coast of Australia about forty-five minutes south of hygiene and approximately one hour twenty minutes north of where all forms of inspiration go to die! Imagine Paris, take away the culture, the art, the amazing food, the bustling metropolis, and the traffic, and then add trees, a beach, teen mums, two preteen stepdaughters, narrow-mindedness, and a Woolies and you're there! (Woolies, think Whole Foods without the deli section.)

There was nothing to do on the Mid North Coast. Nothing. This is the appeal for a lot of people, but I ain't one of those people. I had to do *something* to stay occupied. I was living in the middle of nowhere, pregnant and raising two girls; my hormones were on a roller coaster; and I needed to focus on something to avoid the temptation to pack my shit up and waddle as far as possible away from my situation. So, I decided to not only be pregnant—I was going to throw myself so far into this pregnancy that I would be too busy to do anything other than create life, goddamn it!

I enrolled us into a Calmbirth course, and we quickly became one of those couples who acted as though we had invented childbirth. Calmbirth is similar to HypnoBirthing and Active Birth, and it is fantastic. It's a childbirth education program that prepares future parents mentally, emotionally, and physically.

Calmbirth is all about focusing in on yourself and your partner during the birth, and experiencing the labor for what it is—as opposed to being scared and thinking you need someone else or any intervention. It liberates you to trust and back yourself. I think Beyoncé created it.

I knew my body could do what was needed in birthing a baby, but it was my overactive mind that I feared would sabotage me. I wanted as natural a birth as possible, but I wasn't as free-spirited as I needed to be to facilitate this. When my midwife asked me what sort of birth I wanted, I said: "Ideally, I'd like to have a baby in a rain forest, and by 'rain forest,' I mean 'a place where no drugs are needed and everything is done naturally and in harmony with the surrounding trees and possums,' but the rain forest will need to be heated, with the quiet hum of traffic outside and the smell of culture. Along with this, I'll need an express door to an operating room full of drugs and all the numbing cream in the world if I change my mind, 'K?"

The closest hospital, where I had all my appointments, was a tiny place in a nearby town that had no drugs, no heated floors, very few possums, and definitely no doors leading to operating rooms. It was just a birthing "rain forest": a cold birthing rain forest. And no one wants a cold rain forest. No one. But because of my heart history—now if that isn't a reason to keep reading, I don't know what is!—the doctors were worried that with all the strain on my heart during the labor it could totally explode (this is the official medical-speak). So I was classified as high risk and wasn't allowed to birth at the Rain Forest Hospital. I had to go to the bigger hospital, Drugs Hospital, where they had A-grade morphine and some street-level shit on standby.

The Drugs Hospital was an hour away, so our plan was that we would do all the appointments leading up to the birth at Rain Forest Hospital, and I would do all the tearing and screaming at Drugs Hospital.

I woke up on the morning that my son was due, and I was in labor. We did all the walking around, pregnancy yoga, eating chili, Api wanting sex, and me looking at him with murder in my eyes that is suggested when trying to bring on labor. Api went for a much-needed ceremonial surf, and my mum rubbed my back. All standard "I think I'm in labor" activities.

After a day of "holy shit, can I really do this?" we made our way to Rain Forest Hospital. I needed to get checked to see if I was actually in labor or just experiencing gas (wouldn't be the first time I thought I was in labor but it was just a bad bean burrito repeating on me).

Like I said, Rain Forest Hospital was cold and quiet. I hate cold and quiet. Cold and quiet doesn't calm me down—it freaks me out. Warm and vibrant is what I am looking for when planning a thirtieth birthday or wanting to birth a human. I feel comfort when I know there are things going on around me. I like busy places; I find it easier to relax and "go into myself." No number of lavender candles can relax me like fluorescent lighting and powder-blue gowns and the screams of "IT'S TIME TO PUSH!" coming from the adjoining birthing suites.

Brenda, the midwife at Rain Forest Hospital, sucked. I was in pain, scared, and fucking cold, and she wasn't having any of it. I know I'm not the first person to birth a child and that I didn't invent labor—this is something that we all know was created by Tina Knowles, Beyoncé's mum—but I was scared and was hoping for some comfort and understanding and a possible cup of tea with milk and honey on the side. #labordiva. She couldn't have cared less.

As soon as I arrived she asked if I had had "a show." I went straight into my default setting when I'm uncomfortable and started with some basic gags. Api knew what I was up to straightaway.

Me: Well, depends on what kind of show you're referring to.

Nurse: What?

Api: Oh God.

Me: Well, I've had a number of shows.

Nurse: Pardon?

Api: Please stop.

Me: I've had sold-out shows and critically acclaimed shows, so I'll need you to be a little more specific.

Api: I hate you.

Nurse: Has a big chunk of mucus come out in your undies? A mucus plug? A SHOW?

Me: Oh . . . no.

Nurse: OK, well, I need to examine you to see if you really are in labor.

Me: I'm pretty sure I'm—

And with that she jammed two gloved fingers deep inside me. She retracted them; presented her fingers to me covered in my dignity, self-esteem, and what looked like an oyster; and declared, "*There's* your show." With that she walked out and closed the door behind her.

I looked at Api, and before I could even tell him to "get me the fuck out of here," he was already packing up my stuff. He helped me off the bed and begged me never to do gags in a hospital ever again, to which I declared, "I can't make those kinds of promises, mate. I was just fisted by a woman named Brenda."

We went home, where my mum was pacing, picked up our bags, and made our way to Drugs Hospital. It was a 353,837-hour drive to Drugs Hospital, and everything was Api's fault. The back seat wasn't big enough, Api's fault. My contractions hurt, Api's fault. I was pregnant, Api's fault. The crisis in Syria? Api's. Fault.

Once we got to Drugs Hospital, it was cold and quiet. Jesus, what's with all these cold and quiet hospitals?! We had to ring some sort of bell to get through a few doors, and as soon as we had passed through all of them and got to the birthing suite, it was like a fucking circus and I was so relieved. There were midwives rushing from room to room, men wandering around looking tired and confused, phones ringing, and people talking really loudly. BAM! I was safe; I could totally do this. It still wasn't as warm as I had hoped, but I had to pick my battles—I was about to be ripped from asshole to breakfast. We met our midwife, Wendy, and handed her our birth plan, and she was totally on board with Calmbirth and was super supportive of us wanting a water birth. I know this because she told us, "I'm totally on board with Calmbirth and am super supportive of you wanting a water birth." I was not missing fisty Brenda, that's for sure. Wendy was such an advocate that she started giving Api notes on what was required of him before we even got into the birthing suite.

Wendy: OK, Dad, what Mum will need from you during this amazing process is your support, so during contractions there is to be no touching or talking to Mum, OK?

Api: OK.

Wendy: OK. And, Mum, what I'll need from you is—

I could feel another contraction coming on, I was cold, and I was in no mood for Wendy's anecdotes.

Me: I'll just stop you right there, Wendy. I know what is needed from me, and that's a goddamned human to be vag-shat out of me, so please GIVE ME SOME SPACE!

Contraction over. Possible lifelong friendship with Wendy? In jeopardy.

After another couple of contractions in the same vein, Wendy had to leave us for a while and tend a ward full of fifteen-year-olds who were also crowning. This was good. It gave Api and me a chance to be together and do what we needed to do, that is, him sleep and me walk around the room like an elephant with something to prove.

Over the next five hours I was walking, I was yelling, I was screaming, I was bouncing on the birthing ball, I was kicking the ball, I was in the shower, I was out of the shower, I broke the shower, I was back on the ball, and Api slept. Wendy had come back in a few times to check on me with the phone jammed between her ear and shoulder fielding calls from expectant teenage mothers. Turns out the Mid North Coast is a busy place for damaged hymens and ripening cervixes.

After seven hours of contracting, Wendy came back in and I. Was. DONE.

Me: Wendy, I can't do this.

Wendy: It sounds like you're transitioning, love.

Me: What are you talking about?

Wendy: When it's getting closer to the time to push, most women say they can't do it, but you can, you can, love.

Me: Look, I understand that. I know that people say that they can't do it but they can and they are just scared, but you need to understand that I can't do it! So pack your shit up, we are going home. API, WAKE UP, WE'RE OUT!

Turns out Wendy was right, funny that. I was actually in transition and about to meet my baby. Shit! This gave me no comfort at all. I knew that I was too far along to make the most of the hospital's drug stash, and I quickly realized that the only way I was going to get this baby from the inside to the outside was by way of vaginal exorcism.

I wish I could say that the thought of holding my baby in my arms canceled out any fear I was feeling and instead gave me strength to soldier on, confident and empowered, but it didn't. I was petrified of the pain, the imminent burning ring of fire, and the possibility that I might push so hard that my ass would explode!

Wendy asked me to get on the bed so she could see how dilated I was. I quietly and considerately kicked Api to wake him the fuck up so I might be able to have a woman fist me for the second time that day. And yep, she was right: I was eight centimeters and ready to get into that lukewarm bath and start tearing.

Wendy ran the bath, Api walked around a little dazed—but to be fair, no one wakes up well from an afternoon sleep—and I tried to run out the door.

I got into the bath and nothing changed. I thought that all my troubles would wash away when I got into that water, because that's what the women in the birthing videos tell you. Then there's the women who manage to orgasm during labor. Fuck those women. The water did nothing. I was still in pain, just as uncomfortable, and now I was wet, and not in the way that the orgasm ladies were wet.

My water hadn't broken yet, and I was starting to freak out. The bath was in the corner of the bathroom, and it had a red cord that hung above the center of it in case there was an emergency. It was there to pull on to alert the authorities; then the cast of *Grey's Anatomy* would come running.

Wendy had yet again run out to tend to other cervixes, and I got a crazy amount of pressure in the areas where one would expect to experience crazy amounts of pressure during the transitioning stages of labor.

Holy shit, he's coming; my baby is about to tear out of me without me needing to push! Jesus, were those rumors that the school bitches made up about me being "loose" right?!?!

Then came this almighty surge. "Holy shit!" I screamed at Api. "Get her, get Wendy, he's coming, the baby is coming!"

With that Api jumped up and yanked on the red cord above the bath so hard he pulled the goddamned thing out of the ceiling. While he was trying to untangle the cord from around his perfect face, I realized that it wasn't in fact my baby coming out. It was my water breaking. YES! I'm not loose—suck a fart, Year 8 bitches.

After my water broke, Wendy came back in to check on Api, and I made it my mission to get as comfortable as possible. Trusty Wendy was there to suggest some positions.

Wendy: Try crouching.

Me: No.

Wendy: Sitting back with your legs rested up on the sides of the bath?

Me: No.

Wendy: Some women like to lie on their side, propping themselves up with their elbow, and their partner holds their top leg in the air, like a scissors kick.

Me: No. Please don't say "scissors kick."

Wendy: OK, let's get you on all fours.

Api: Hee-hee, that's what got us into this.

Me: ARE YOU SERIOUS?

Api: Sorry, I was just trying to lighten the mood.

Me: Come here and let me cut your dick off. That will lighten my mood!

So I got on all fours and bit the metal on the side of the bath, and the pushing began. They say that you should push into your bum when having a baby and it makes you feel like you are pooing.

Well, Wendy had this covered. I was forty-five minutes into pushing into my bum and Wendy, my Wendy, leaned over and said how important it was for me to really focus on pushing like I was pooing.

Wendy: We're nearly there, we really are.

Me: FUCKING ARSE TIT PRICK POO AND MUTHA-FUCKING BALLS!!

Wendy: You're doing so well, Mum.

ME: AAARRRGGGHHH!!!!

Wendy: Now, just keep focusing on pushing into your bum. I don't want you to worry if you do a little poo, as I have a poop scoop.

With this she presented a poop scoop shaped much like a ladle and showed it off proudly, much like Mufasa did with Simba in *The Lion King*. She put it next to my face, she showed it to Api, and then just for added value she showed it to me one more time.

This was all going on while I was mid-contraction. I turned around—well, my head turned 180 degrees and the rest of my body didn't move. I glared at her with bloodshot eyes and snarled through gritted teeth: "I'm not interested in the poop scoop, Wendy. I don't care if I shit on your face. Just. Get. Him. Out."

Api was scared. The trainee midwife standing in the corner staring at my shirtless #hothusband in the bath was scared. I even scared myself. But Wendy didn't flinch. She didn't take her eyes off me as she slowly put the poop scoop down. I think if she could have, she would have told me to shut the fuck up and know my place, but as she was a professional she let it slide. Wendy and Celeste's BFF status was back on track.

An hour into pushing, Wendy said they needed to monitor my heart, as they didn't want it to be straining for too long. Turns out that being in active labor for eight hours is fine, but once you hit that eight hours and five minutes mark, people start to panic.

It was around this time that the burning ring of fire was really in full flight and Wendy could feel the top of my baby's head. GROSS! She asked if I wanted to reach down between my legs and feel his head so I could be a part of this moment.

A PART OF THIS MOMENT? I *am* this moment. Without me there's no baby head, there's no #hothusband crying in the bath, and there's no poop scoop. THERE *IS* NO FUCKING MOMENT! But I get FOMO real bad and I didn't want to feel like I was being left out of my son's birth, so I reached down and it was as gross as I had expected. It was gooey and hairy and fucking weird.

I gave myself a "hands where I can see them" rule and continued grunting.

With another massive push, his head tore out. Because I was on all fours I couldn't see him, but Api could, and he said our son looked exactly like him and immediately started to cry. I was like a cat trying to get comfortable on a leather couch in an attempt to bend around and see my baby, but as the rest of his body was still inside my body, I wasn't as agile as I would have hoped. So I just had to trust Api.

A little birthing-in-the-water trivia: babies can stay underwater for ages before they need to draw their first breath, and it's the atmosphere around them that pushes oxygen into their lungs, so when my son stayed immersed in water for a full minute between me pushing his head out (gross) and the next contraction when his body came flying out, and I was screaming, thinking he was drowning, it turns out he was fine. When the rest of him came shooting out, I caught him, held him on my chest, rearranged the umbilical cord that was conveniently wrapped around my thigh, and never let him go.

We named him Lou.

I now have two beautiful boys, Lou and Buddy. They are by far the best thing that has ever happened to me, second to that time I met Sporty Spice.

The One Where I Discovered Ritalin, My Childhood (Not So) Imaginary Friend

I come from a small family; it's just the four of us—Mum Kath, Dad Nev, my older sister Olivia, and me.

My parents are such a great team. Mum has a short fuse, and Dad loves nothing more than ticking her off, in a loving way of course. Mum is really creative: she has run three successful interior design businesses and at the ripe old age of sixty-two decided to start up her own soy candle brand, Flame Candles, supplying wholesale candles to shops across the country. My dad is the handiest and cleverest man in the world. He is funny and patient and can fix anything. Between them they have built two houses—Mum designed them and Dad built them—had two daughters, and put a lot of effort into naming their pets as though they were a barren couple and their pets were all they had. When I was born we had a silky terrier, Phoebe Josephine; then we got a schnauzer, Lucinda May, followed by another silky terrier, Bronte Isabella, and Mum is currently treating her second schnauzer, Clover Lee, like a misunderstood genius child.

Liv and I were lucky kids; we never went without. We had our own rooms, we could eat cheese whenever we wanted, and when we were annoying—and our parents sent us outside because we were being too loud—we had enough outdoor area to whip sticks at each other without doing any real damage.

I wasn't really great at school—it just wasn't my thing. Every now and then I'd pretend I had slipped into a deep coma, so when my dad came in at exactly 6:55 a.m. EVERY SINGLE MORNING to get me up for school, I would squeeze my eyes shut and go as stiff as a board, behavior commonly associated with coma patients, so I wouldn't have to go.

I just kind of hated the idea of it. I struggled academically, I couldn't concentrate, I was bored easily, and I just wanted to do anything other than having to stay still. Turns out I had ADD, and a small private Catholic school on the Far North Coast of New South Wales just wasn't a good breeding ground for these "symptoms."

I love making people laugh—at me, with me, whatever. As long as people are laughing because of me, I'm happy. At school, I was the perfect scapegoat for my mates, who liked to mess around, and also a good victim for teachers to unleash on. Math, English, PE—basically any subject that didn't require a microphone—were my least favorite. I remember science was the most painful.

We had to line up outside before each science class. All our bags had to be left outside, so we would get our books out and walk in single file past our teacher, who was standing at the door to see if she was happy with how we were standing. If she was satisfied with our posture, we were allowed into the classroom.

I was usually at the back of the line with my two unsuspecting partners in crime, Sean and Doug. They would have their stuff all ready to go, especially Sean—he was a really smart dude who Doug and I would playfully tease to make ourselves feel better.

On this one day, as I've always been a clusterfuck, I was probably asking to borrow a pencil from a girl who was already annoyed at me and not listening to anything being said to me. As we were filing in, Mrs. Science put her arm up in front of me. I thought she was looking for a high five, or at the very least a fist bump, but I soon realized this wasn't the case. She was "dealing with me."

"I'll just get you to wait outside, Celeste," she said, without making eye contact.

"What for?" I protested.

"We could do without the distraction today." And with that she closed the door.

The rest of the class filed in, including Sean and Doug, and I watched them longingly, much like the way Rose looked at Jack when he slipped off the door in the middle of the North Atlantic Ocean at the end of *Titanic*.

I was so embarrassed, but because this soon became her standard practice, I learned how to channel the shame.

But really. Distraction? You think not allowing me into the classroom, and leaving me outside with everyone's bags and a wall of windows through which EVERYONE can see me, would stop me from being distracting? I guess not all scientists are smart.

For a comedian, being sent out of class before it even started because of the risk of being distracting is like Bill Cosby being given free Rohypnol and a private suite at the Plaza. If I had an unobstructed view of Sean and Doug, then shit got really real.

For these kinds of impromptu performances, I had a few standard gags that were my staples. The elevator traveling down and pretending to be pulled offstage were my go-tos; they always got a laugh. Pretending to be attacked by a bee was another crowd-pleaser. Or, if I could get someone's attention while Mrs. Science had her back turned, I'd mime asking them a question through the window, and when they responded I'd mime, "I can't hear you." It brought the house down.

The main attraction was my disappearing act. When Mrs. Science turned around to see what everyone was laughing at, I'd jump to the ground, out of sight, buried in everyone's bags. Eating people's unattended food was the payoff.

I wasn't a naughty kid; I was too scared to be naughty. I was just loud—loud and funny—and most of my teachers didn't dig it. But I was OK with it. If anything it helped me. It helped me work on being a funnier lady, a stronger lady, and a more resilient lady.

Being diagnosed with ADD (or maybe it's ADHD: I can't really remember, I wasn't paying attention) was the greatest thing that could have ever happened to me—well, that and getting tickets to Janet Jackson's '98 *Velvet Rope* world tour. (People say *Rhythm Nation* was her greatest album, but I'm telling you *Velvet Rope* had everything: badarse beats, haunting ballads, and enough Auto-Tune to turn any of the straightest ladies gay.)

I always had the best intentions. I would organize to study like a boss. My parents had set up a study area for my sister and me, and I'd get my pens out and put them alongside my schoolbooks. My calculator was in prime calculator position, and I'd even write up a study timetable, using every colorful pen at my disposal. Red for math, pink for drama, and then I didn't care about the rest. The timetable would be stuck on the wall directly in front of me.

I'd have a lovely glass of room-temperature water ready to go, and I'd pick up my pen, keen to get my study on, then . . . that would be the end of it. I'd be distracted by something, anything. The dog walking past, an unfolded towel in the corner of the room, my mum sneezing from the neighbors' living room—anything would catch my attention and I'd be out of there. This, my friends, is what us professors call "classic ADD behavior." I had all the best intentions to sit and do work, I was even excited about buying all the stationery and desk accessories, but I just. Couldn't. Do. It.

Mum and Dad took me to see a specialist when I was sixteen in the hope of getting answers. Even though I totally had boobs and had been bleeding monthly for approximately two years, I still had to go to a children's doctor. The waiting room was full of toys and copies of *Spot the Dog*. There were posters on the wall featuring the letters of the alphabet, with pictures next to them: *A* for *Apple*, *B* for *Butterfly*, and so on.

As I went through the letters, enjoying the distraction from the doctor smell of the waiting room, they all seemed to make sense—yep, *K* is for *Kite* and *L* is for *Lion*—until I got to *Y*. Next to the letter there was an unassuming photo of a boat. A blue boat with white bits. The word under it started with *Y*, but I couldn't figure out what boat starting with *Y* was spelled like that. I turned to my dad and asked, "What's a *yak-a-hat*?"

The receptionist looked over her desk with an "oh, bless her, this must be a hard struggle for you, Dad, having to deal with such a challenging daughter" look on her face. Dad looked at me and through tears of laughter said, "It says *yacht*."

"Well, why the hell isn't it spelled properly?"

"Good question, princess. I don't know." My dad's my biggest fan—well, just behind my mum, who is a close runner-up to my sister.

If the doctor had overheard this conversation, it could have saved my parents a lot of money in doctor's fees, as he would have given me the tablets right there on the spot and I would have been on my merry way, feasting on Ritalin sandwiches.

When I went into the appointment, Mum, Dad, and I sat in three chairs that were all in a line. My chair was closest to the doctor, as I was the main event. Here is where I learned that ADD is hereditary and is commonly passed down to the child by the dad.

Holy shit, didn't this make sense?! My dad and I are exactly the same! I wondered if this information would upset him. I looked over to him and saw that he was focusing on a fly that was wedged between the glass window and screen and realized he'd probably be cool with me being the heir to that particular throne.

Mum did most of the talking during the appointment, and I was asked a lot of questions. Even as an outgoing sixteen-year-old, I still looked to my mum for the answers.

I was given a series of questions.

Q: Do you find it hard to concentrate?

A: Can you please ask me again? I wasn't concentrating.

Q: Do you find it hard to read, write, and spell?

A: Know, not raly.

Q: Do you think you have a short attention span and are easily distracted?

A: Sometimes, but—hey, did you just see that bit of lint fall off your sweater onto the floor?!

Q: Are you constantly in trouble at school for being slow to start work and for never finishing anything?

A: Not telling.

After the appointment, the doctor asked me to wait outside while he talked to my parents about what steps to take to "move forward." I think he just needed to see what sort of drugs he had on hand, as I needed that shit in my system stat!

I sat back out in the waiting room, chilling with five-year-olds who called me "lady" and not really thinking too much about what had just happened. The doctor's office door was left open; I think he wanted to come off as a cool doctor who appeared approachable while prescribing drugs that keep overweight truck drivers awake for forty-eight hours. I could hear the entire conversation.

Mum: We don't want her to change.

Doctor: These drugs won't change her—they will help her.

Mum: Good. We know she is full-on and loud, but we like that. Her personality isn't a problem; it's her struggling to concentrate that is making things hard for her.

Dad: How long do you think that fly has been trapped in there?

Doctor: Ritalin doesn't alter personalities—it will just help her focus.

Mum: OK, great. I just want school to be easier for her.

Dad: Do you think the fly has family who are worried about its whereabouts?

Mum: Neville!

Dad: Sorry.

Mum: We will commit to this medication only if it helps her to feel better about being herself.

Doctor: I really think this is the best option for Celeste. It will only have a positive effect.

Mum: OK, great.

Dad: I'm hungry.

I'll never forget that conversation. As a loud, full-on, average-looking girl, the fact that from a young age my mother was so passionate about me being me meant everything. I also think about that fly.

When we got home I was straight into the drugs, and they were good; they were so good. They kicked in straightaway, which is what you're looking for in top-shelf gear. I sat on the couch, opened a booklet on "Living with ADD," and read a paragraph out loud to my parents. It went a little something like this:

> *Childhood symptoms of ADHD include poor impulse control, hyperactivity (i.e., cannot sit still), difficulty focusing on immediate tasks, and inability to pay attention to instruction. Children with hyperactivity-impulsivity often have difficulty forming and maintaining friendships and receive poor conduct evaluations due to their inability to behave appropriately in school. These children seem to disregard common social courtesies by repeatedly interrupting conversations and speaking out of turn.*[3]

I looked over, and Mum and Dad were crying. It must have been such a validating moment for them as parents, knowing that they had made the right decision, and the results had been immediate.

"I can't believe you just read that. You have never sat still long enough to read anything, ever," said Mum through tears. Turns out reading the first page of *The Baby-Sitters Club*, then skipping to the very back page and skimming the last paragraph doesn't count as reading a book. Pfft, technicalities.

We went camping every year with a group of family friends.

---

3   See www.healthyplace.com/adhd/adhd-children/
what-is-add-and-adhd-add-adhd-definition/.

There were six families in total, all of us knowing each other to varying degrees. In one of the families both parents were teachers. They were strict, and I don't think they really liked kids, which is fair enough. Kids can be shit, especially when they are all together in a classroom and they hate you.

On the camping trip before the diagnosis (sounds like a blockbuster movie: "Coming this summer, *The Diagnosis*, starring Celeste Barber and Winona Ryder"), I was being an arsehole and my poor parents were at their wits' end.

My mum confided in one of the teacher parents: "We are going to get Celeste tested for ADD. I think it will help if we can possibly get her onto some medication."

To which the teacher parent responded out the side of her mouth while looking around to see if anyone could hear her: "Leave her with me for six months, and I'll get it out of her."

This broke my mum's heart. Turns out not only kids can be arseholes; some teacher parents on camping holidays can fit pretty comfortably into that category too.

After the sweet, sweet Ritalin started flowing through my hungry veins, life got SO much easier. I could actually sit still and concentrate. I had one and a half tablets three times a day, and it was a routine that I fucking loved. At 7:30 a.m. with breakfast the pill popping began. When the bell went for recess at 11:30 a.m., round two was underway, and when it was home time, I would walk past the bubbler (*bubbler* is what us Australians call a drinking fountain, but you know that if you live in Massachusetts, Rhode Island, or parts of Wisconsin), throw down the final hit for the day on the way to the bus, and Bob's your uncle, I'm a fucking scholar.

Ritalin suppresses your appetite like nothing else, so I was never hungry. As a result, I lost a shit ton of weight, which as a sixteen-year-old girl gains you a shit ton of respect (sad face emoji).

Breakfast would consist of a chocolate milk and a Cheesymite scroll. (Anyone outside of Australia needs to get onto these. They are a bread roll baked with cheese and Vegemite, and coupled with a warm Milo they have the power to make all the bad feelings stop.) Did I mention I have the palate of a seven-year-old?

Lunch was a Zooper Dooper, and then I was done until dinner, when I would pick at whatever my mum had made.

OK, let me unpack that for you guys.

Vegemite is a spread that you put on toast. It must be applied to toast ONLY after the butter has been applied and has melted so much that the once-crunchy toast now runs the risk of wilting due to the amount of said butter. DO NOT try Vegemite on its own. If you do, we can't be friends.

Milo is a chocolate crunchy delight that you add to milk, miss the shit out of it, then chug it.

Zooper Doopers are icy poles and come in such flavors as fairy floss, candy, and your childhood. That's only if you had a good childhood; if not, I'm sorry for being inconsiderate.

Ritalin was a lifesaver for me; however, I didn't tell any of my friends, and I only told one teacher when I started taking it. He wasn't even a teacher of mine; he was the year coordinator and I was happy telling him, because I didn't ever see him. I didn't want to be looked at as sick. Different, sure, I like people thinking I'm different, but not less than. I was petrified of anyone knowing I had ADD, let alone having to be on a drug for it. I remember one time thinking the cat was out of the bag when a weird-looking guy who I was friends with said he liked me, so I told him a dick joke to get out of awkwardly telling him I wasn't interested, and he was so pissed off that he started scream-singing the Jackson Five's classic "ABC, Celeste has got ADD!" at my face in front of the surfer boys at school, who all thought it was hilarious. But they also laughed at my dick joke so, you know, you win some, you lose some. Turns out he didn't know I had ADD; he was just a prick. I didn't mind being called names, but I was sure that everyone knew I had a "learning difficulty." It was exhausting being so secretive about it, so I turned it into my secret superpower. By day (unmedicated) I was just loud, disruptive, quick-witted, sassy, and opinionated, but by night (medicated) I was loud, disruptive, quick-witted, sassy, opinionated, *and* could concentrate for longer than 0.05 seconds. Now, if that isn't a story line for a new Netflix show, I don't know what is.

A friend of mine has been advised by teachers that she look into getting her seven-year-old son put on Ritalin. She's freaking out. The first question I asked was, do these teachers go on camping holidays and generally hate kids? After she assured me they didn't, I told her that I think seven is *way* too young to be going on any sort of behavioral medication. Kids are flat out trying to sit still for an entire five-minute episode of *Peppa Pig* (aren't we all!), let alone six hours a day listening to the same teacher talk about numbers and letters. Of course they are going to get bored, child! (Spoken in RuPaul's most sassy voice.) I'm a little torn with the timeline of my diagnosis—part of me thinks if I were diagnosed earlier, school may have been easier. But then I think if I was on the drug from as young as seven, I wouldn't be as resilient as I am. And that resilience was needed so much through my life (ohhh, yes, that's another little nugget to keep you sexy little bookworms reading). If I was medicated from a young age, I would have thought that I was just normal and that everyone was on drugs or some sort of "help me learn" stimulant. But because I started later than what is considered "normal," I knew I wasn't normal; instead, I knew that I was a little different, and different is interesting. Different is the tits![4] It didn't stop me from getting into trouble. My mum's concerns that the drug would change me were unfounded, as I was still a loudmouth and smart-arse, but I could also concentrate long enough to let someone finish what they were saying and then come back with a kick-arse comment instead of interrupting them.

I thought once I left school I would never get into trouble again, except from my nana, who always had a problem with my posture. But I was wrong: getting into trouble still happens to me in my adult life. I seem to attract it—not getting-bashed-up or having-drug-dealers-feel-me-up kind of trouble—just if there's naughty shit going down, or someone is going to make an arse out of themselves in public, I'm usually at the epicenter of it. I noticed from a young age that I had the type of personality people either loved or loathed. I don't look for it—it just happens.

In my early twenties I started taking an antidepressant, Zoloft. I can't remember why I went on it; I think as I had just graduated from drama school and a lot of emoting was involved, I thought I was broken and needed to be medicated. I remember feeling a little bit weird mixing Ritalin and Zoloft. I wasn't just feeling weird about it emotionally and metaphysically, but I was literally feeling fucking weird. I was having anxiety attacks and struggling to string thoughts together that didn't involve negative self-talk coupled with a lot of hysteria.

---

4   Ritalin changed my life at sixteen, because I was given the space by my parents to be a kid for sixteen years. School was fucked for me, but I had sixteen years to be a kid and sort my shit out. Putting kids on drugs because they can't sit still or because they are a bit naughty and talk back to the teacher can be dangerous. Give them time to properly fuck up and be kids.

Api and I had been dating for about six months, and we were having a fancy breakfast at a fancy café in Sydney when I had a major panic attack. I felt like the poached eggs were out to get me and the overpriced coffee was sitting on my chest like a pregnant pig. I couldn't breathe or talk. Api didn't miss a beat—he took me home, fed me lollies (not a euphemism), and avoided direct eye contact. (Lollies = candy. You know that, right?) This was when I realized that Ritalin and Zoloft weren't the cocktail that I had hoped for. I went to the local shrink located next to an animal rescue—so I trusted him with my life—as my usual shrink had an appointment with her shrink, in Mexico. I told him about my weird feelings and asked him what "metaphysical" meant, and he said that I was the "least depressed person" he had met and suggested I come off the drugs and see how I go. I started this process, which is very similar to pushing shit up a hill with a sharp stick. It's horrible and, at times, hard. Turns out if you try something twenty years later and expect the same outcome, then you're an idiot. I continued on for a few years drug-free. When a close friend died, my world fell apart. I decided that I needed to go back on Zoloft, and I have been on it ever since. Leading up to my 2018 US tour I wanted to try to go back on Ritalin because I felt as though my workload was getting on top of me, and I was a grade-A clusterfuck and wanted to get my shit together. I spoke to my doctor about the effect Ritalin has on adults and if it's OK for adults to take Zoloft as well or if the drugs still aren't friends. I was advised that mixing the two still wasn't an awesome idea. So I tried again to come off Zoloft in preparation for Ritalin in the hope of falling back into the awesome routine I had established as a teenager.

Turns out that wasn't to be the case—I know, I'm as shocked as you. Trying to come off antidepressants while planning a US tour, looking after two young boys, moving one teenage stepdaughter out of the house and another one in, writing a book, and dealing with dying friends and parent-teacher interviews is dumb dumb dumbity dumb. I thought I was onto it, and the bottle of wine I was consuming nightly wasn't self-medicating; rather, it was an easy alternative. When I talked to a friend about my new hopes for Ritalin coming back into my life and kicking Zoloft to the curb, he politely and smartly reminded me that I'm fine as I am and that I should just continue being a cluster-fuck because everyone who knows and loves me has accepted it. That I should just get on the acceptance bandwagon and keep on keeping on and stop trying to shake things up.

So that's what I'm doing. I'm just accepting what I've got and getting on with it.

The One about My Dad

I've never really asked my dad if he wishes he got an official diagnosis and subsequent medication, because I think I know the answer: "I'm fine as I am, princess. If I can last this long without it, then why would I start now?" Well played, Neville, well played.

My dad is everybody's mate; everyone loves a bit of Neville Barber—"Nifty," as he's affectionately called. If he's not making you laugh, he's laughing at you not laughing.

There are three certainties about my dad.

He Doesn't Share Food

Dad: If you want some, I'll buy one for you.

Me: No, Dad, I just want a bite.

Dad: Well, I'll buy you one and you can bite that.

Me: But I don't want a whole lasagna, I just want to try some.

Dad: Well, I do want a whole lasagna. That's why I bought it.

Me: Are you serious—you're not sharing with me?

Dad: Deadly.

And with that he will set up a barrier around his food, made up of salt and pepper shakers, sauce bottles, and glasses, while firmly holding a knife in his hand as a weapon.

He's the Originator of Dad Jokes

Neville Barber's go-to joke:

> *A grasshopper walked into a bar and the barman said, "Hey, we have a drink named after you." And the grasshopper said, "Really? An Eric?"*

And that's it, that's the fucking joke. But it's not about the joke; it's about the joy he gets in telling it. He doesn't usually tell jokes to make you laugh. He tells jokes—well, to me and my sister anyway—to annoy you. If he knows he's onto a winner, he will repeat it over and over, breaking the main rule of comedy: "Don't treat your audience like idiots."

Dad: Get it? The grasshopper's name is Eric?

Me: Yes, Dad, we get it.

Dad: But the bartender meant he has a drink called a grasshopper.

Me: Yes, Dad.

Dad: But what the bartender didn't realize is the grasshopper had his own unique name.

Me: DAD! FUCK.

Jackpot!
Neville 1, the Barber daughters 0.

He's Always Ready First—ALWAYS

When we were kids, if Mum said we were leaving the house at 6:00 p.m., at 5:45 p.m. Dad would be sitting on the couch with the car reversed out of the driveway, air-conditioning running, cooler bag of lemon, lime, and bitters,[5] and a nice bottle of white wine for Mum. He would wait patiently for her as she figured out what perfume to wear from the collection he had bought her over the years, and for Olivia and me, who were fighting over whose acid-wash drop-waisted skirt was whose.

When we paraded down the stairs at 6:05 p.m., Dad would always greet us with a compliment. "You look lovely, dear," he would say to Mum. "You look lovely, girls," he would say, continuing the compliment. Then we were in the perfect-temperature car and off!

My dad is solid like a rock, always there for anyone and always happy to tell you a dumb joke that you will roll your eyes at, then excuse yourself from the conversation to go to the toilet and record

---

5   Nifty doesn't drink, never has—except at my wedding in Bali, when two days before the Big Day, we were by the pool and I opened a bottle of vodka that was infused with gold and was a gift to my soon-to-be groom from my sister and bro-in-law. Dad asked for a shot of vodka, and didn't this get the party started. We all had a shot; Dad requested a second one straightaway, followed directly by a cup of tea and a three-hour sleep. Like I said, Nifty doesn't drink.

the joke in your phone so you can recite it to your friends later at the pub.

He was an only child and lived in the same house from the day he was born to the day he and Mum moved in together. Dad lived on a dairy farm, and when the local milk carrier would come by at 7:00 a.m. to pick up the milk, he would also pick up Dad and take him to school. The school was so small that on a number of occasions the principal would call Nana Rita to make sure Dad was going to school that day, as no one had turned up and they needed him there to keep the school open. He was four.

As Dad got a bit older, he would ride his bike to and from school along a dirt track every day. Once he got home from school on a Friday afternoon, he wouldn't see anyone apart from his mum and dad until he was back at school on Monday morning. If a car went past, the family would go onto the balcony to watch the big display. He kept himself busy, no dramas, no complaints.

His dad, Harold, was a tough man, old-school, didn't show any emotion. Nana Rita and Dad were a team. And when Dad met Mum, Nana took her in as the daughter she'd always wanted.

Dad was super close to his mum. Rita had wanted more kids, but Harold wasn't into it, so in those days that was that. I reckon my dad would have LOVED a sibling or ten, but he will never tell you that, because that would be complaining, and that's something Neville William Barber doesn't do. He's grateful for his life and more than happy just to go with the flow. He's a master at keeping busy and not imposing his time on anyone for any reason.

My dad works as the maintenance guy at a private hospital on the Gold Coast, a job that started as a one-week gig in 1996, and because he's so excellent to have around and good at what he does, the hospital just keeps creating work for him.

He's so loved that when he was in the hospital the second time in his life (the first time was the time he was born), the staff put him up in the presidential suite and there were nurses who weren't rostered on that day visiting him to make sure everything was OK. (He had tightness in his chest, which freaked everyone out. Turns out it was gas. Classic Neville.) My mum, who has been in and out of the hospital her whole life due to dodgy lungs, is lucky to get a bunch of flowers on her hospital visits these days, whereas Dad gets a full-blown fanfare if he gets even as much as a blood test.

When I moved out of the house at seventeen, my dad wrote me notes of encouragement on the back of business cards. Every time I would go back home, or he and Mum would visit me, he would have a fresh business card with a fresh note of love and encouragement. The business cards have been replaced with official and professional texts.

> Celeste
> Just looked at e mail from the copy editor Just another
> one of your talents
> You never stop surprising us all
> Just more acknowledgment for the great person you are
> Love Dad xxxx

The One Where I Danced a Lot

I danced when I was a kid, and when I say danced, I mean *danced* (tilts head with an over-the-top click of the fingers). I danced at eisteddfods (think *Toddlers and Tiaras* with a lot less hair pulling and a lot less lipstick), at shopping centers, at school fairs, the Ekka (the Royal Queensland Show), conferences, football grand finals (by football, I mean Rugby League—think NFL with a lot less shoulder pads, a lot less money, but the same amount of male privilege), in my nana's shower, in *my* shower, and given the chance I'd dance in *your* shower too.

I was a self-proclaimed unique triple threat: I could dance, Dance, and DANCE. And I loved it.

My mum said that I could dance even before I could walk, but as I have said one billion times, my mum exaggerates a bit. This didn't stop me from telling anyone who would listen, especially my fellow dance enthusiasts. You know those conversations you have with like-minded twelve-year-olds about how you were born to do this and no one has the experience or dedication that you do?

"*I* know all the dance moves to EVERY one of the Spice Girls' songs, even 'Viva Forever,'" Julie would say over Macca's while we sat in the splits (Macca's is what we call McDonald's in Australia because we are lazy but cool).

Elissa would chip in. "Well, *my* big sister has taught me all the steps to *all* the senior dances, *and* she said that if any of the senior girls can't do the end-of-year concert, then I can *totally* step in because I'm *so* good at learning all the steps."

I looked at these girls, knowing full well that what I was about to share with them would stop them dead in their flexible tracks. "Well, *I* could dance before I could even walk."

Pause. Silence. Nothing. "Aaand my uncle's a firefighter."

They smiled. BAM! I knew it would floor them.

I danced at the Johnny Young Talent School (JYTS) on the Gold Coast. When I started there, it was the Colleen Fitzgerald Dance School. Then Ms. Colleen married Mr. Lance from JYTS and they merged the dance schools.

Look, I won't lie: it was hard at first to accept the merger, but when the job opportunities came rolling in thick and fast to dance at Jupiter's Casino on the Gold Coast because we were now known as part of THE JOHNNY YOUNG TALENT SCHOOL DANCERS (this must be sung, never just spoken, using jazz hands), we got over our loyalty pretty quickly.

I was fifteen when I went on my first interstate trip to Darwin for two weeks and performed in shopping centers. There was a group of us that went, some as dancers, some as emcees, and some as suit operators. (You know those larger-than-life characters that walk around shopping centers during school holidays, scaring the piss out of all the kids? Well, there's an actual person inside them, not just fear and misery.) In Darwin, I was lucky enough to be the suit operator of Sonic the Hedgehog, a rabbit, and one of the Simpsons—I want to say Marge, but I think it was Maggie. Given it was the September school holidays in Darwin, and the average heat at 8:00 a.m. was 37 degrees Celsius (I think that's 7,865 degrees Fahrenheit, but don't hold me to it), I managed to halve my body weight in a week while still eating two-minute noodles forty-five times a day. We all stayed in hotel rooms with balconies and would sun ourselves first thing in the morning because "morning sun gives you the most even tan." This was my first and last interstate tour, as I think my mum was worried that I came back after two weeks of work with protruding neck bones and a dependency on MSG.

I grew up near a beach that has bred some of the best professional surfers in the world, but it was lost on me. I didn't do weekend nippers (a bunch of kids on the beach every Sunday during summer wearing weird hats learning how to not drown—an Australian rite of passage) like everyone else because Saturday was dancing day—DANCING DAY—a day to dance: DANCE DAY! Mum would drop me off at class by 9:00 a.m., and I would carpool home with James Corden, singing the Spice Girls' greatest hits, and since James wasn't available, our neighbors Esther, Bianca, and Ashleigh were my lift home.

Jazz for the babies (two to four years old) was first, and Bianca and I, along with other Show Group and senior dancers, were student teachers. I didn't love teaching, but I just loved being at dancing, and especially on Saturday because it was when everyone from all the different studios across the Gold Coast would come together. We would compare the choreography we had learned that week and share clear nail polish to cover up the holes we made in our shimmers (stockings with a high-shimmer finish, you guys: shimmers). We weren't one of those dance schools that had to wear a uniform; we could wear whatever we wanted, as long as it was awesome and outshone the other dancers. One of the male dancers, who wasn't "out" yet, was partial to a fluorescent-yellow unitard—an outfit that he would reserve for a 34-degree day (pretty sure that's around 5,643 degrees Fahrenheit), knowing he would sweat and would make all the other curious boys jealous.

Ms. Colleen always wore black, black on black with a side of black and something black. She always had a full face of makeup that my sister would say looked as though she had laid it out on her bed, tied her hands behind her back, and just fallen face-first into it. Ms. Colleen did a few tours of Vietnam entertaining the troops in the '60s—something that she loved and romanticized about often. She was a born performer and gave us and the studio everything she had, including her bad temper and sass.

After Babies Jazz came Babies Tap and a whole lot of noise. Intermediate classes came next, and this is where it got exciting, because all the older dancers would start arriving and stretching or trying on costumes for upcoming shows. Then there would be a break where we would run down to the 7-Eleven to get a medium Slurpee and a Killer Python that we shoved in the straw of the Slurpee so it would freeze. Killer Pythons are life! Think Twizzlers, shape them like a snake, and give them lots of different colors and flavors and treat them like the perfect food pyramid you wish they could be. Ms. Colleen would put in her order of a cheeseburger with no bun, a can of Coke, and a chocolate, which the most responsible dancer (a.k.a. her favorite) would get for her. I was never asked.

Then it was back to class and our turn, the Show Group and Seniors. This is when we would TURN IT ON. We performed like we were at Madison Square Garden and JLo was our backup dancer. Well, I did anyway—I didn't really know what the others were doing, as I had my eyes closed most of the time to get the full effect.

Dancing was a place full of super-weird people that I felt safe with. Mr. Fluorescent-Yellow-Unitard was super bendy and loved to tell me inappropriate stories about his sex life. He called everyone the *C* word before the *C* word was even a thing. At first, I thought he just called me that as a nickname—a term of endearment, if you will. But then I found out otherwise and was equal parts flattered and confused.

If I wasn't meeting my potential in any aspect of my life, he would challenge me and ask why. He would laugh at my jokes and roll his eyes when I complained that the prettier blonde girls had been put in the front row *again*.

"Listen, C, you will never be in the front line. Ms. Colleen has her favorites and you're not one of them. I love you. Get over it."

"But I've worked really hard."

"No one cares. Now, let's sit in the sun and bitch about absolutely everyone."

Dancing was the first place, outside my family, where I felt safe being loud, ambitious, and different.

Ms. Colleen died recently at the age of seventy-seven, and I will always be grateful to her for teaching me how to count to eight and for playing show tunes so loud that I think it has caused me permanent damage.

The One about My #metoo Stories (Sad Face Emoji)

I'm a big supporter of the #metoo and #timesup movements. I'm pretty vocal about standing up for women's equality and that crazy idea that women shouldn't feel as though we need to be subjected to sexist bullshit just because we're women.

I have a #metoo story—two, in fact—and I'm going to share them in this book because I want to. I'm not going to name people because I don't want to. These are *my* stories about *my* experiences, and even though they have in no way shaped who I am as a person, they are still my stories.

I've noticed that when people are named in #metoo stories, then *they* become the focus. Taking them down becomes the main objective, and the person who has told her story becomes just another victim and just another woman with a grudge. The perpetrator becomes the focus and is treated as a one-off event, whereas it's a whole culture that needs to change.

I'm putting these stories in black-and-white in my book because I want other women and girls to start doing or not doing things because they do or don't want to—not because they feel that they should or that it's their responsibility. The only people in these horrible situations who have any responsibility are the men. A responsibility not to sexually harass, assault, bully, or intimidate women at any point, in any field, for the rest of time. In the name of the father, the son, and the holy goat, amen.

In 1996, my fourteenth year dancing and fourth at the Johnny Young Talent School, I was given a solo in the end-of-year concert. I was the only senior and only one in the Show Group—the fancy dance group—who hadn't been given a solo before, but this year was *my* year. You better believe it. I'd pinned that curly headpiece into my head year after year, but this year was different; I didn't even cry when it drew blood. I was ready—I was fucking born ready for this solo, damn it!

Ms. Colleen would put together a medley of different musicals each year. And by "put together a medley," I mean she would pick her favorite songs from her favorite musicals, cram in some tried-and-tested choreo from previous concerts, and not give two shits about the narrative or how she was butchering classics. AND WE LOVED IT!

Only the Show Group dancers were invited to take part in this section of the concert. One year it was a song from *Grease*. Julie, the pretty blonde girl, played Sandy; Remi—the only straight guy, whose mum and dad redefined the term "stage parents"—played Danny; and I was a fun Pink Lady double up in the back, miming the wrong lyrics to songs and trying to make my friend Bianca laugh. Another year saw us do a number from *West Side Story*. Julie, the pretty blonde girl, played Maria; Remi, the only straight guy—whose mum and dad redefined the term "stage parents"—played Tony; and I'm pretty sure that was the year I was lucky and talented enough to play a little bit of all the ethnic characters up in the back.

Then in 1996, my final year, we did part of the 1966 classic *Sweet Charity*, and I was cast as—wait for it, you guys—THE LEAD. Yass, queens, I was cast as Charity Hope Valentine in *Sweet Charity* (hair flick emoji).

One of the awesome things that went with such a prestigious role as being a fancy Show Group dancer and performing in a bastardized medley was the exciting and nearly impossible quick changes that needed to be performed side stage. They were almost as important as the concert itself. And they involved A LOT of planning and responsibility. The job of organizing other people's props if they were onstage was given to Show Group performers only because they knew the importance of it all. Most people who had solos didn't have to organize anyone else's props, because people who had solos in the concert were looked at as heroes, like doctors or Paula Abdul.

Ms. Colleen: I need a dancer to run the umbrella from one side of the stage to the other during the final chorus of "Singin' in the Rain." Celeste, can you do it?

Me: Oh, I can't, Ms. Colleen. I have a quick change side stage and only just enough time to get back on for . . .

Looks around, clears throat, and waits for everyone's attention.

Me cont.: MY SOLO!

echo solo solo solo.

If you had to do a quick change side stage, you needed to get your shit together weeks before the concert was even in your visiting aunt's and uncle's diaries. You had to assess if the best time to "set" your QCC (quick-change costume—keep up, you guys) was before the concert even started or if it was better to leave it until you had a break between routines while the three-year- olds were doing their tap number to *Swan Lake* (my dad's worst nightmare). Another vital step was to let people know where you were putting your things so no stage mum with an agenda would come along and sabotage your preparation.

My mum had made the costume for my solo this year. It was a simple black leotard that she had got a local swimwear designer to make, but it had a bit of a twist. Mum had designed the costume with a sheer diamond cutout in the center of my chest/belly, and she had alternated black and silver sequins around the perimeter of the diamond. For my solo, I would wear this fancy little number, paired with some tan chorus shoes and a red feather boa, naturally.

It was after I'd performed my solo, "If My Friends Could See Me Now" (HELLO! Art imitating life!), that my super-fast, super-important quick change would take place. Ms. Colleen had put the Show Group's big number, "Big Spender," right after my fancy dance solo, so I had to get moving. I mean, I couldn't stay on stage for my solo AND a group number, because a fifteen-year-old performing "Big Spender" alongside other thirteen- to seventeen-year-olds in front of dads, uncles, and begrudging family friends in THE SAME high-cut costume as for her solo, well, that would just be weird and make everyone uncomfortable.

So, in stepped Kath Barber once again, with her handy sequinning skills. The device normally used for a QCC was a tearaway (a piece of clothing that is held together with a piece of Velcro—think the Chippendales but with more body hair). There was usually a skirt that was added or taken from a costume for a quick change. Only, you guys, mine wasn't a tearaway. My mum thought of it all! It was a Lycra skirt that I could just step into during the ever-important and overemphasized quick change. The skirt had a tiny slit on the front right side, which she had also sequined in alternating black and silver, in keeping with the whole theme of the night: *my* night.

I was SO focused on my solo, and just as focused on the placement of the black Lycra-bedazzled skirt and split-sole jazz shoes I would wear in "Big Spender." I had decided that I would place my skirt and jazz shoes on the ground just offstage.

Two years earlier, our end-of-year concert had been upgraded from the local services club down the road to Jupiter's Casino on the sunny

Gold Coast, and it was next level: a full-blown casino that tourists and rich old men looking for foreign wives would flock to. I'm not sure if it was because we were now the official Johnny Young Talent School that we were treated to end-of-year concerts at the casino, but I think the dance school's namesake and the casino were as dodgy as each other, so it just makes sense.

Each year we would have a different emcee for our concerts. One year it was Humphrey B. Bear (think Dumbo or any other mute children's character that is a stupid choice to host a concert), another year it was Ms. Colleen's son Brad, and another year it was our singing teacher. I always dreamed of being that emcee; I thought of this position as being much like when a *Saturday Night Live* cast member comes back to host, something I really wanted and aspired to do.

This year we had some random old local entertainer. I'm sure he was a great pimp back in the '20s, and what seemed like the natural progression of his career was to then host nightly trivia on cruise ships and emcee at kids' dance concerts.

So, my costumes were set, I had just finished—sorry, SLAYED—my solo, and I ran offstage, dodging my fellow not-so-professional teenage dancers as they made their way on with chairs and random feather boas, and looked for my carefully placed gear.

It was exactly where I left it. YES, let's get busy!

As I raced over to my things, adjusting my clipped-in wig, I noticed there was a stool placed over my stuff. No problem: I'll just reach under said stool, grab my costume, throw it all on, and be back onstage for the opening bars of "Big Spender"—front and center where I belonged, goddamn it!

It was at this point that I realized the emcee, a Big Fat Talentless Old Man, was sitting on this stool, preventing me from getting what I needed. (Oh, what a metaphor for life as a female.) The Big Fat Talentless Old Man was talking to the owner of the dance school; I wish I could say it was Ms. Colleen, as she would have put a stop to what was about to happen, but unfortunately it wasn't—it was another Big Fat

Talentless Old Man, and the two of them were having a jolly old time side stage at a kids' dance concert. When they saw me approaching, they smiled at each other, and the emcee spoke to me.

Big Fat Talentless Old Man: What's wrong, sweetheart?

Me: Um, I need to get my things.

BFTOM: Where are they?

Me: Um, they are under the stool.

BFTOM: Oh, I see.

And with that he looked at the other Big Fat Talentless Old Man and smiled.

I could hear the beginning of "Big Spender"; I needed to get my stuff and get the fuck out there. When I realized what I needed to do to get my things and the smug looks on their faces, I froze. The emcee stared at me as he sat back in his stool—the fucking stool that was preventing me from getting to my things and my career! He crossed his arms, spread his legs open as wide as his creaking old hips would let him, and slid his crotch forward on the stool.

"Well, you better get down there and get them, sweetheart."

I remember thinking, "You've got to be kidding me." I walked slowly to the stool, feeling both their eyes on me, and instantly felt sick.

When I got to the stool, I bent down to get my things as quickly as I could, and he spread his fat, short legs farther apart and slid his crotch farther forward on the stool toward my face and groaned, and the other Big Fat Talentless Old Man laughed for a second time.

"Fuck you," I wanted to say. But he was a man, and I was a female child. But fuck you!

As soon as I grabbed my stuff I thought, "Brilliant, I'm done. I can quickly get changed and get the fuck out of here and tell my dad all about it after the concert so he and my uncle Ray"—who wasn't even at that concert but would have made the seven-hour trip—"can beat up these two predators."

However, as we weren't performing at the O2 Arena, even though we acted like we were, there wasn't a lot of room side stage, and I quickly realized that this exploitation wasn't over. It had, as I was about to learn, only just started.

I realized I had nowhere to change except directly in front of the fat, groaning, objectifying men. I felt a wave of fear come over me. I had to either miss my dance—a dance that I was so excited about, *my* fucking dance—or get dressed in front of these two pigs, who seemed to delight in making a fifteen-year-old girl feel uncomfortable, unsafe, scared, and as though it was her job to entertain them.

I kept my head down and got changed as fast as I could. They were staring at me the whole time. The only time they broke their stares was to wink at each other. I focused on the music onstage, knowing the quicker I ended this involuntary performance behind the black curtain, the quicker I could get out onstage and perform in the light.

I got my skirt on, changed my shoes, and ran onto the stage four bars into the song with tears in my eyes.

Tears soon turned to sweat as I danced my heart out, completely forgetting about what had just happened, to the point of thinking I had made it up and it hadn't really happened at all.

The One about My Fake Brother, Michael

In the first house we lived in, Dad built Liv and me a Costume Room off the back of the garage to keep all the dancing costumes my mum had sewn for our not-so-lucrative-yet-overenthusiastic careers as entertainers. It was awesome.

For my sister and me, the Costume Room was a magical place. It was where our two worlds collided.

Growing up, Olivia and I were completely different. She was cool and independent and ate thirty-seven apples a day. And even though she was clumsier than a newborn trying to ride a unicycle, she was fearless.

Walking home from school one day, she said, "If I ran fast enough, I could totally jump over that four-foot barbed-wire fence," and with that she ran full-force into said fence, which resulted in a busted knee, a trip to the hospital, and twelve stitches.

She recently tested out her agility by trying to ride a skateboard, an obvious choice for a thirty-six-year-old who trips over uneven grass.

"Can I borrow your deck and have a roll?" she asked Api one summer's day.

"Sure, mate." He is her biggest fan.

She jumped on that board like she was a seasoned pro. As the skateboard took off down the hill with Olivia atop it, laughing her head off, my darling Api was running alongside her, experiencing fear that only Olivia should have been feeling. When it was starting to get a bit crazy, he said, "All right, Livvo," (that's what he calls her) "when you're ready just jump off, keeping your weight even."

"Sweet!" she screamed with excitement.

Of course, being a Barber she did the exact opposite. She took more of a one-footed flying leap off the skateboard, and as she was midair, under his breath Api said, "Oh fuck! Not like that."

She hit the ground like a sack of shit.

Mum, Dad, and I didn't flinch, as this was a common occurrence.

But Api was worried, and strangers who saw and felt the thud were concerned too. People ran over to see if she was OK, and a lovely homeless man who was sitting nearby offered her his walking stick.

I'm pretty sure Olivia laughed so hard she farted.

I'm a lot more precious than my sister. I wouldn't be caught dead on a skateboard; I'm flat out trying to swing myself on a swing set without freaking out. I'm scared of everything. I check the bath for sharks, and even mentioning the word "snake" has me lifting my feet off the ground and placing them higher than my head.

This is a red rag to a bull for my sister: pissing me off was her job description as a teenager, and she was bloody good at her job. She's the funniest person I know; she can laugh at herself like no one I've ever met.

Whenever Olivia and I see each other she still wants to wrestle me. Partly because she knows she can beat fifty shades of piss out of me, but mainly because she knows I'm going to scream her name, "OOOLLLIIIVVVIIIAAA," like Oprah does when she introduces a celebrity, while I throw my arms around like a helicopter to keep her away from me.

We went to different schools most of our lives.

Olivia went to the local public school and was cool and awkward and fit right in. I was more challenging and needed a smaller school with more attention. So I was off to the local private Catholic school that had only been open for a year.

Not surprisingly, we weren't the best of friends growing up, as I didn't understand the Keanu obsession (I was more of a Jonathan Taylor Thomas kind of gal), and there were only so many times she could tolerate me screaming at her through tears: "You just don't get it, Olivia! The Spice Girls ARE better than the Beatles!" But I loved her the regular little sister amount. Over the years we have become really close, super close.

We talk to each other at least five times a day, have been known to have Skype dinners with each other and our families (we live in different states), and have entire conversations only using dialogue from *Bad Boys*.

Even though we didn't have much in common as kids, we would hang out in the Costume Room Dad built us and talk about everything from which Corey she would marry, Feldman or Haim, to how plausible it was for me to wear the wedding dress from the "November Rain" music video to my own wedding, "because I really want to play to my strengths and show off my legs." I was eight.

I remember a specific day in the Costume Room that changed my life forever. Olivia was using a blunt pencil to carve the lyrics of "Riders on the Storm" into the chipboard floor, and I was wrapping myself up in tulle, humming "Anything You Can Do, I Can Do Better," when she dropped a bomb.

Olivia: Hey, I need to tell you something.

Me: OK, want to make up a dance first?

Olivia: No, this is important.

Taking the sequined bowler hat off my head, I was all ears.

Me: What's wrong?

Olivia: If I tell you this, you have to promise not to tell Mum or Dad that I told you.

WARNING: If an older sibling says they have information they want you to know but you can't let your parents know you know, run for the fucking hills with your fingers in your ears screaming: "NOT LISTENING, BITCH!!!!"

Me: OK.

Olivia: You have to pinkie-promise not to tell ANYONE.

Me: Fine.

Liv: And if you keep the promise, I'll let you sleep in my room for a whole week.

This was just getting better and better: a pinkie promise, street cred from my big sister, AND permission to sleep in her room for a whole week. Let's do this!

We pinkie-promised and I braced myself for the biggest moment of my life.

Liv: Ready?

Me: You betcha!

Liv: OK. We have a brother.

I froze. I slowly put the tulle wrap back on the rack, next to the sequined bowler hat, and walked over to her without blinking.

Me: UM, WHAT?!

Liv: Yep, we totally have a brother. His name is Michael.

Me: Where is he? Is he upstairs?

Liv: He's dead. He died of a terrible disease.

Me: Oh my God! What?

Liv: He died of leukemia.

Me: I don't know what that is.

Liv: It's blood AIDS.

I started crying, I was so sad. The thought of having a brother was awesome, and I was so invested in this idea; then hearing he had died, and of something as terrible as blood AIDS, I mean, you can't make this stuff up.

Liv: It gets worse.

Me: How?!

Liv: When Dad built this Costume Room, he knew we would love it and be here most of the time.

Me: Dad's so nice.

Liv: So they buried Michael under the Costume Room so we would feel connected to him.

And with that she smiled, walked out, and closed and locked the door behind her, leaving me in there on my own with dead fake Michael's ghost.

That was the last day I ever went into the Costume Room. Mum would be up all night beading our costumes, and I loved sitting and watching her, imagining myself dancing around wearing her intricate craftsmanship, but as soon as Mum asked me to quickly go down to the Costume Room to grab something for her, the dream ended. I would refuse, point-blank. It broke both of our hearts.

I love my sister more than I thought possible—she is my most favorite person in the world (well, her and Prince Harry)—but whenever we meet someone named Michael or Michelle, I need to take a deep breath and a big step back and remind myself that my sister is blood, and there's no way I would survive jail.

The One Where I Was Bullied at School, I Think

I was bullied at school, I think.

See, this is one of the great things about having ADD. I don't have a very good attention span, so when people at school started talking smack about me I'd hang around for the first part, the big opener: "You're such a dumb slut." But by the time they got warmed up I was already halfway to the swing set, chasing a squirrel I thought I had seen three hours earlier. So I think a lot of it was wasted on me.

The word "bully" gets thrown around a lot. Much like the word "empowering" (when a rich, topless model poses on her dad's yacht on the French Riviera she's not "empowering," you guys, she's spoiled). Or when my teenage stepdaughter says she will "literally" slit her wrists if her three-year-old brother calls her Bum Bum one more time, again it's not really an accurate description of what is going on.

See, sometimes people are just shit. They can be mean, they can be hurtful, and they can sleep with your boyfriend when you're out of the room trying to help a friend who's vomiting. You can be called names or, even worse, be ignored. But this isn't bullying. This is just people being, well, shit.

I think we need to be careful about how we use the term "bully." A guy once told me I have a face people don't like. He said it a few times, and in front of a few different groups of people; there was a lot of laughter, and a few people repeated it to strangers, who also got in on the joke. It was mean, unkind, and a little hurtful, but I don't think I was being bullied.

Ruby Rose has spoken about her time at school, and it sounds horrible, terrifying, and downright wrong (see https://www.news.com.au/entertainment/ruby-rose-bashed-by-classmates/news-story/d7b979864ccce14ca9a9cdd45d9c7011):

> *There were five girls and one boy who picked on me badly. They followed me all the time after school, just yelling abuse at me. I would get so petrified I'd just run home—I never retaliated.*
>
> *I never cried in front of them. I think that made it worse. They were determined to break me. Sometimes they would just come up and punch me in the head, but there was a lot of intimidation.*
>
> *I almost preferred to be bashed rather than just threatened, because at least it was over and done with.*

This isn't teasing or kids being mean. This is downright bullying.

I had a disjointed group of friends at school. I didn't really have my ride-or-die bestie that I couldn't live without; I was a bit of a bed hopper with friends. I get bored with people easily, so I needed to move around, get different things from different people. Well, that's when I was younger anyway. Now I have the same six friends, and my books are closed when looking for new people to come into the group.

Some were friends from primary school, some were new friends I made at high school, some were dance friends, and some would laugh at something I did once, so they instantly became my best friends.

I remember one girl who didn't like me. Well, that's putting it mildly—she hated my stupid dumb guts and wanted to beat the crap out of me. It was kind of weird, because it seemed like an overnight hatred, as I was friends with her sister (Friendly Sister) and even though she was hotter than the usual sun, I never had any tricky feelings toward her (Sexy Sister).

These sisters could not have been more different. Friendly Sister was fun and sweet.

Sexy Sister didn't like girls who were friends with boys, and she wanted boys to like her and girls to be jealous of her. In Year 7, when I was trying to navigate my way through a swimming carnival wearing a maxipad with wings under my swimsuit, she was sporting a white crocheted string bikini (keep in mind we were at a private Catholic school, and our school swimsuits looked a little like something one would expect to see on *The Handmaid's Tale*), and it would be fair to say her wish came true: the boys really started to like her, and the girls were jealous as hell. #blessedbethefruit. She was the first one in the grade to wear a bright-pink lacy bra under our thin white cotton school blouse and flick her hair in a way that defied gravity. When I stayed at their house, Friendly Sister and I would be forced to watch Sexy Sister model bikinis, as she wanted our honest and unbiased opinion.

On top of being banging hot and pulling off tissues as swimwear, Sexy Sister was super smart. She was in all the top classes and was one of those people who did really well at school without having to try. Damn you, Sexy Sister!

I was loud, insecure, and made people laugh, and Sexy Sister didn't like that. She didn't like my personality and she wanted to do something about it, to teach me a lesson.

In hindsight, I feel Sexy Sister didn't actually hate me or want to "beat the crap" out of me, but it gave her a new type of attention, that of a hot girl who can karate-chop the funny girl, and that seemed appealing to her. Whatever blows your hair back, love.

I arrived at school one day and there was a lot of buzz around, well, me. Someone came up to me when I was only five minutes off the bus, excitedly telling me that "Sexy Sister is going to beat the shit out of you."

"What? When? Now? But why?"

I turned around to get back on the bus and get the hell out of there, but Dennis the bus driver was a stickler for being prompt and had already left. Come on, Dennis!

"No, at lunch. She said you're a fat clown and everyone hates you."

"Surely that's not a reason to want to bash someone?"

"She wants to teach you a lesson; it's going to be huge!"

"All right, mate, calm down. No one's teaching anyone a lesson outside of Mr. Gazel's math class."

"Well, she said she's going to do it on the oval near the basketball courts at 1:20 p.m."

"So specific."

"Yeah, the bell for lunch goes at 1:10 p.m. so she's giving everyone enough time to get their lunch, get a drink, and go to the toilet if they need to before they head down."

"How considerate."

"You know her dad is a martial arts champion."

"Jesus, of course he is."

The deliverer of bad news ran off, fist pumping the air like he had just delivered a *Game of Thrones* spoiler to his archenemy.

"Shit. Fuck. Tits and arse. Why the hell is this happening? This must be a mistake. Surely she has got me confused with some other loud, academically challenged, attention-seeking girl named Celeste Elizabeth Dominica Barber. Does she really want to bash me?" Oh God, how does this go down? Would I walk down to the oval at 1:19 p.m. (I think in situations like these it's important to be prompt) and try to talk to her?

The Clown: Hey, mate.

Sexy Sister: I'M GOING TO BEAT THE SHIT OUT OF YOU! MY DAD IS A MARTIAL ARTS DUDE.

TC: Really? I thought he worked in the Thai restaurant at the beach.

SS: Shut the fuck up. It's on.

TC: On? What's on?

SS: IT. IT'S on.

TC: Hang on. Why? Why are you so angry at me?

SS: Because. (Adjusts boobs in bikini.)

Awkward pause.

TC: I like your earrings.

SS: Thanks.

TC: Can you please not bash me? I'm freaking out.

SS: OK. Can you please tell all the boys that I'll do nearly anything?

TC: Um, OK, but I think they already know.

Is that how it goes down? Or do I just cop it, let her punch me in the face? Oh God, I really don't want to get punched in the face, and I bruise like a peach. Or is it a hair-pulling type of thing, or given her dad's martial arts background am I looking down the barrel of fly kicks? Fark! Do I stretch before? Maybe I could tell her some sort of joke and everything will be OK. Yep, that's what I'll do. I'll drop a Barber-style dad joke to create a distraction and run as fast as humanly possible to the library. (Note to self: find out where the library is.)

The whole morning, I played it cool. I thought if I just acted like it wasn't a big deal, then it would go away. When people asked me about it EVERY TWO SECONDS, I wouldn't lift my head from my work, acting relaxed: "It's all good, nothing's going to happen. I don't know what she's even talking about."

Then lunchtime came. The bell went at 1:10 p.m., and people ran out of their classrooms. They pushed out of the class doors like the people in Japan shove themselves onto overpacked trains. They ran and got their lunch, grabbed a drink, and started running down to the oval (she was quite considerate to allow that time).

I packed up my books slower than a sloth on heroin. My heart was beating hard in my chest, and I felt tears streaming down my face. I was petrified.

Mr. Gazel, the greatest math teacher in the history of numbers, asked if I was OK.

"Yeah totally, I'm like totally fine and OK." He gave me a kind smile and left.

I walked out into the quad, and it was like a ghost town. There were a few late kids running down to the oval, shoving past me and shouting "you're going to get fucked up, Barber" as they passed.

Fuck fuck fuckity fuck, this was it.

When I got down there with my friends, I could tell they were nearly as freaked out as I was; we were running around like idiots, and we were all talking about boring, mundane stuff in really loud, over-the-top voices. Because that's what you do when you're facing immediate death and don't want to let on that you're scared shitless.

Me: Why do you think Ross is so obsessed with Rachel?

Friend 1: Because she's amazing.

Me: You're right.

Friend 1: So anyway, my face totally couldn't believe the color of the sky.

Friend 2: Yeah, me either.

At 1:35 p.m. (fashionably late: classic pretty-girl behavior), Sexy Sister came down to the oval with a posse of bitchy prepubescent sexy siblings, who had determined looks on their faces that put feminism back forty years.

My friends and I saw them, along with the rest of the school, and like a deer in the headlights we froze, staring.

Friend 1: Oh fuck, is she going to do it now?

Me: Jesus.

Friend 2: I'm freaking out.

Me: YOU'RE freaking out? I think I just soiled myself.

Friend 1: Me too.

With that they took off. They got out of there so fast that Friend 1 even managed a cartwheel as part of her exit. I don't blame them; I mean, I'm a loyal friend, but if the roles were reversed and someone wanted to bash one of *my* friends, I'd like to say I'd stay by their side to the bitter end, but that would be a big, fat lie.

There I was, alone and sweating. I started to walk back up to class; I thought that if I just kept my head down and walked past her, she would see that I was weak and leave me alone, and I was fine with that. I was OK with looking "weak" or "scared"; I just didn't want to get punched in the face or, worse, fly-kicked in the boob.

As I came side by side with her she stopped in her tracks.

"Breathe, Barber, just breathe," I said to myself.

I was just about past her when she launched herself at me, pretending to throw a punch. I flinched and, like a bull at a gate, took off out of there so fast I farted.

As I ran up to the library I could hear everyone laughing. I knew what they were laughing at. Me. They were all laughing at me. I didn't care. I knew I looked like an idiot, and I didn't care. When Sexy Sister launched herself at me, it had been so subtle that I doubt anyone but me even knew what had happened. But I was so petrified it felt like Mike Tyson had just swung at me because I'd petted his pet tiger without asking.

I thought I should have been brave and looked her in the eyes, let her know she couldn't intimidate me. All the antibully advice that we are given is to show that you're not scared, that no one can intimidate you, that you're the boss of your own destiny, and if you confront the bully, then they will back down, right?

Well, I didn't want to. I was scared and I wanted to run away; I didn't care if this made me look weak. If this made it seem as though I was backing down and she had in some way "won," good on her. If this was winning to her, I'd happily emcee the medal ceremony at a reduced fee.

My gut had said get the hell out of there, so I'd backed myself and did exactly that.

I ran past the science labs, searching for the library. I looked over my shoulder to see if she was gaining on me or if her henchmen had weapons they were planning on throwing at me, but no one was there. Everyone had remained on the oval, pointing and laughing at me. I didn't care; I kept running.

As I stumbled through the doors of the library, I heard some teachers trying to swap their lunch duty so they could go and "watch the show." Right in that moment I knew I had made the right decision. I wasn't at that school as entertainment. Sure, I'm happy to make people laugh, but fuck that.

I had heard so many people throw my name around over the course of the day—"You're fucked, Barber"; "Oh God, Celeste is going to get smashed"—that I got all *Rain Man* on myself and felt I needed to reclaim my name. In the deserted library, I pulled out a pen and some paper and through tears started writing my name over and over again. "Celeste Barber. Celeste Barber. Celeste Barber. Celeste Barber." After writing this over and over I signed off with "is the best, chuck out the rest."

This was around the time when the two most popular girls in school also hated me. Jeez, when it rains it pours. Having the power that comes with high school mean-girl status, these girls managed to get the entire Year 8 class to ignore me for the whole school year. Well, that's an exaggeration; they didn't get everyone to *completely* ignore me. There were daily "no one likes you, you dumb shit" and "shut the fuck up, you ugly slag" comments thrown my way across busy play areas while I sat alone compiling monologues and writing jokes.

I arrived on the early bus and would walk up the long entrance to our school, under the massive cross that overlooked us all. #underhiseye.

But this particular day was weird. Janet, my latest unofficial bestie, was there but not keen to talk, and considering we had been on the phone the night before talking about the pros of moving from pads to tampons with applicators, I was a little thrown.

"Are you OK?" I asked, confused.

"Yep," she said as she briskly walked off toward the two popular girls.

Not one to let something go, I walked up to another mate, asking if Janet was shitty with me, to which they responded, "I don't know, you'll have to ask her."

I was starting to get nervous. "I just did, fuckface! What's going on?"

This mate walked off to join the cast of *Mean Girls* too, and I was left alone. I tried to ignore them. But you'd have more chance of me growing wings and cycling to the moon on a hamster than ignoring something. I marched up to the group, my heart beating up into my double chin, and they all started giggling and looked at their feet. Classic arsehole behavior.

"What's going on?" I said in a shaky voice. I was ignored.

Shit.

"Have I done something wrong?"

Bitch 1 turned around to reveal her large forehead and responded out the side of her small-lipped mouth: "Fuck off, no one likes you."

Everyone laughed. WHAT?

Now, I'm not innocent, not innocent in any way. I'm not someone who says something to keep the peace. If you piss me off, I'll tell you.

But this was next level. In that moment, all my mates changed; they went from fun and kind to scared and mean. I know kids and teenagers can be shit—trust me, I'm a stepmother to TWO teenage stepdaughters. But these bitches were being bitches just because they could.

After this embarrassment, I walked away. I'm no fool; I was used to being a part of the joke but was not comfortable being the butt of it.

I walked straight back down to the buses to greet my friend Alyssa, whose bus was always the last one to arrive. Alyssa was a hippie; we called her Sis because she was like a sister to everyone. She was sweet, kind, and always smelled like home. Alyssa would have my back, or at least stand next to me while others tried to stab me in it.

She got off the bus, and much like when you hit your head at school and you say you're fine, then the school calls your mum and as soon as you hear her voice you start to cry, when I saw Alyssa I broke down. I was so sad.

"Everyone hates me," I said through tears and a shaking voice.

She said nothing, just kept walking with her head down. "Sis?" I caught up to her, panicked, and walked alongside her.

"I don't know what's going on. Janet isn't talking to me, and Debbie just told me to fuck off."

"I don't want to talk to you," Alyssa said, not lifting her head.

Oh God, I felt sick. Sis was everyone's friend. She became student body president, and rightly so; she was lovely and smart and kind. So when I saw that even *she* wasn't talking to me, I knew it wasn't going to be a fun time.

I was confused. I racked my brain—what the hell had I done? Had I talked smack about someone behind their back (when a prepubescent teenager does this, it's punishable by death)? I couldn't think of what I could've done to warrant such anger and hostility from every kid in the school.

So, in that moment down by the buses, I took a deep breath, pulled myself together, and made a decision. I just decided I didn't care. I didn't care to investigate; I didn't care about begging for forgiveness for something that no one was going to help me understand. I realized all people wanted was to make me feel like shit, and I didn't care. I had bigger stuff going on. I had drama monologues to learn, *Friends* episodes to watch and rewatch, dancing concerts to show off at. These bitches were the least of my worries.

This continued for an entire year. Bitches 1 and 2 had used their mean-girl power to persuade everyone in Year 8 into thinking I was a loser who wasn't worth talking to. If anyone talked to me, they were grilled by the bitches about why.

Over the next year I could count on one hand the people who didn't abuse me.

I have to give credit where credit's due: these girls must have put in a lot of work to get everyone onside. This was before emails and texting, so I'm not sure how they got the message out or kept it going over the school holidays. Letterbox drops? Chinese whispers? I guess there were sexual favors in return for screaming shit at me, but I'm just speculating. It was a big job, and one they pulled off (pardon the pun) successfully. Well done, arseholes.

People say when you're getting bullied the best thing to do is walk away, ignore it. This will show the bully you don't care, and they'll get bored and leave you alone. The usual advice is that your actions will then affect the bully and they will hopefully back down.

I say walk away because YOU don't care, because YOU are bored with it. Who fucking cares what impact it has on THEM! Sort yourself out and forget about them.

My friend's daughter is copping a lot of shit at school at the moment, and despite wanting to march into the school and make heads roll, I told her to focus on herself—not because it will show the haters that she doesn't care, but because she is worth focusing on, and it gives her the power and opportunity to find out who she is and what she wants.

It's so hard—I get it, trust me, it's fucking hard. But you need to treat it like a rite of passage, a voluntary, self-inflicted rite of passage.

On the second to last day of Year 8, Bitches 1 and 2 had decided I was worthy of acknowledgment and they *allowed* the rest of the class to start talking to me. Great! The horrible feelings of loneliness and dread had gone, but it didn't change me—I just had more people to talk to. That's not to say it didn't affect me, because of course it did, but looking back on it I don't remember it being the main experience of my school years. Because *I didn't care enough about what they thought.*

I knew what I wanted to do with my life and I fucking did it, and the cast of *Mean Girls* tried to get in my way and make me focus on them and their bullshit, but I didn't care enough. I wasn't interested in their shit. The crying and the changing of schools that my parents had suggested all played a part in character building, but the way they treated me didn't shape who I am. Only Nutella can do that.

I remember around this time overhearing someone say that your school years are the best years of your life and thinking, "Well, if this is the case, I'd best make my way to the bathroom and fashion some sort of noose out of my tie, because if this is as good as it gets, I'm out."

But I knew it wasn't. I knew I was ready to get the fuck out of there and start smashing the whole personality-gets-you-places thing. I don't advise going and trying to get people to bully you in the hope of building character, but I do advise that *if you are being bullied, or people are just constantly being punks to you, then get busy.* Get your shit together and focus on what you like. If you like handball, get a tennis ball, find a brick wall in the quiet part of the school, and play until the bell goes. If you like chess, focus on whatever it is that chess players focus on. If spelling is your thing, then GET SPELLING, YOU AWESOME LITTLE NERD! Don't fucking worry about them, because God knows they are more interested in you than you should EVER be in them.

Just back yourself, and if you want to run scared and cry under your bed for six weeks because that's your safe place, then DO IT. Don't worry about what lessons it will teach the bully or what message you are sending the world. It's not your responsibility to take on these things—it's your responsibility to look after yourself.

And if it doesn't let up, send me a message, I've got an army of over four million who will happily come and kick their arse for you.

P.S. Sexy Sister now runs a successful health and lifestyle blog about kindness and living your truth. She also writes columns on how important it is to look good and what it was like to be bullied at school. Bless.

The One about Falling in Love with Comedy

The school bitches were hurtful, but it never threw me off the scent of working toward who I wanted to be and what I wanted to do.

And it was around this time that I first fell in love with comedy.

Everyone loves comedy, right? We all love laughing at people when they fall over, or when someone voices the inner monologue of what goes through a dog's mind when it's licking its own anus. I mean, we all love that stuff, right?

But I mean it was around this time I *really* fell in love with comedy as an art form.

It was a Tuesday in 1995, and I had only a handful of friends because of the two *Mean Girls* wannabes—ah, the power of the bitchy, insecure vagina.

Friends was on Monday night at 7:30 p.m., and it was my favorite show ever. I loved the banter, the setups, the chemistry, and of course the hair. I loved it so much that I based my friendships and daily exchanges around it. (Maybe *that's* why I didn't have friends, not because of the bitchy vaginas—hmm, interesting.)

I loved WATCHING *Friends*, but I didn't SEE myself in it, so I didn't understand how I could do any more than just admire it like the rest of the world. (Well, the rest of the world except my mum, dad, and a guy I went to university with.)

I never thought I could ever be on a show like that other than as a talented extra at Central Perk, sipping pretend coffee and bathing in the shadow of Gunther. And I was totally fine with that; I was so happy just to enjoy what I saw and wait my turn to be a funny extra and just work on my talents as a tap dancer.

I have always been loud and full-on, and it's kind of fun for, like, five minutes. People will look to me to fill silences when a new group of friends is hanging out, and I'm the one who will banter with the sassy retail assistant and end up getting everyone a 10 percent discount. But then it can get old and, well, full-on.

On *Friends*, I saw three really pretty ladies playing really pretty, clever, safe, and "what is to be expected of ladies in comedy" characters, only I didn't know it at the time. I wanted to be on the show; it was on my bucket list along with seeing the northern lights, being interviewed by Oprah, and meeting Beyoncé's twins.

But I was too big, in both the physical and character sense, and I was at the age where transitioning from training bra to underwire was a real emotional roller coaster and took up most of my time (shout-out to my DD and above ladies!), so I had a lot on my plate.

Every Monday night I would finish dinner early and make sure I was in front of the VCR (for my millennial readers, google it; it'd be too hard to explain without pictures and judgment) with a fresh VHS tape at 7:15 p.m. ready to press "Record" at 7:29 p.m.

I would record *Friends* while watching it. I think that this act alone proves my dedication: no millennial would stuff around with the VCR during an episode of *Vampire Diaries*, get the timing just right to catch the opening credits and theme song, and be present enough to pause out the ads but make sure each scene was recorded in its entirety so as not to miss any Phoebe and Joey comedy gold. No way! They are too busy sending dick pics to their boyfriend's best mate, which is an art form in its own right.

I still put it on in the background for company when I'm home alone.

Then on Tuesday morning I'd get up early, get my shit together for school, and rewatch the entire episode (sans ads because they were cut out, obviously) so I could have the dialogue down pat to recite to my handful of friends who hadn't been scared off by the bitchy, insecure vaginas. (Shout-out to Doug and Sean for being my weekly audience.)

Some people can do the worm or roll their tongue, but not me, not *this* little sitcom buff. *My* party trick was reciting every single line from *Friends*, with the accents, the inflections, and the Ross-inspired dramatic exits. I can also do a mean Running Man and will do Old Lady Dancing at the drop of a hat.

I remember getting off the bus this particular Tuesday morning and walking the usual walk down the long concrete footpath toward the massive cross as I recited the previous night's scenes in my head, laughing at just how spot-on my accent was. I walked up to Sean and Doug and unleashed the scenes on them, so just a normal Tuesday. Only today they weren't into it.

They would usually laugh at my reenactments (Doug more than Sean) as we walked together to roll call. But this Tuesday was different. Doug still laughed at what I said—he was always the best audience— but Sean couldn't even look at me.

Oh well, maybe he was just in love with me—isn't that what we're supposed to tell ourselves in high school? "If he's rude or mean to you, then he's totally into you"?

(NB Fuck that. I am currently teaching my boys that if you like a girl, you bloody well tell her. You let her know that her hopes and dreams—whether they are to become the first female president on planet Mars or to sell detox tea on Instagram—are VERY important to you! And if things become as serious as she wants them to be, that you will actively wear "The Future Is Female" T-shirts and respect her decision to wear and express whatever she wants, whenever and however she wants. My oldest son is six.)

But no one was in love with me; it turned out the insecure vaginas had gotten to them, and I was on the outer. They'd cast me aside like Beyoncé did the fourth member of Destiny's Child. This killed me—not because they had fallen victim to the cast of *Mean Girls* but because not even my comical attempts could cut through, even if they *were* uncannily like the original. This was the day everything changed—well, for me anyway. I'm pretty sure it stayed the same for the other girls, the bitchy insecure vaginas who, as Katherine Ryan would say, are "not normal but ordinary." But for this little Ritalin-induced comedian-in-the-making, it all changed. Barber got focused.

Quite partial to a dramatic exit, I stormed off to the drama room, my mecca, knowing that my tried-and-tested set was wasted on these now-horny ghost friends.

When I arrived in class my brilliant drama teacher, Sharon Singleton, was a better audience than I could have ever hoped for. She always encouraged me to be weird and loud, and she made sure I kept being weird, loud, and as full-on as often as possible.

After a successful recap of the previous night's episode, I got ready for another excellent drama class with my even more excellent drama teacher. It was one of those lessons that started off better than you could ever have expected, with Ms. Singleton wheeling in a TV and VCR. YES! Video lesson! We all sat on the ground and watched as Ms. Singleton cracked open the video and with her back to us loaded it into the VCR.

Then four words came up on the screen that changed my life forever. ACE VENTURA: PET DETECTIVE.

I sat staring wide-eyed at the grainy TV and watched one of the greatest comedic actors in history, Jim Carrey, in a piece of comedy art. We didn't just watch it, we studied it, and I obsessed over it, over him.

It wasn't until I saw Jim Carrey that I discovered what I wanted to do. It completely blew my mind.

From that moment on I realized I wanted to be an actor and comedian, and that now I could be. It was OK to be big, loud, over the top, full-on, and brave. It was better than OK—it was fucking awesome! Something Ms. Singleton drummed into me for years.

After the film ended Ms. Singleton asked what we thought Carrey based his character and mannerisms on.

I threw my hand in the air like a missile, responding, "Animals! His mannerisms are like animals!"

I remember this not only because I'm in love with Jim Carrey and this film but also because Ms. Singleton said I was right, and that doesn't happen much (violin emoji).

And that was that: I was sold. I had thought comedy was just a bit of fun and a bit of stupid, but I realized in that moment on the navy-blue plastic carpet of the drama room at Saint Joseph's College that I could be on TV and in movies being funny, and not just as an extra on *Friends*.

So I hung up my tap shoes and got focused.

I wanted to do more, more of everything. Mum and Dad arranged for me to do acting classes outside of school, and it was great.

The classes were once a week and were about a forty-five-minute drive from where we lived. I would get a lift there and back with a guy named Harry who was also doing the classes. Harry was about seventy-five and bloody loved a good acting class.

On our ninety-minute round trip Harry and I would talk about the classics. He would tell me what it was that made Shakespeare really stand out from the rest, and I'd give him my detailed analysis of why I believed that Joey and Rachel's relationship was problematic (not that it needed much explanation [eye roll emoji]).

The classes were a bloody hoot. Like any good acting class, we were given a number of scripts to work on, all from well-known movies that none of us were suited to or would ever be considered for. Much to Harry's disgust, there were no Hamlet soliloquies among the handouts, so after week one he started bringing his own.

I remember always being given the comedy scenes and loving it. I found them really easy and exciting. I always played the funny characters, the fun, kooky characters who were usually played by older, big and bold, mostly musical-theater actresses. Bette Midler in *Beaches* and Muriel's sister in *Muriel's Wedding* were two of my favorites.

As I was one of only three females in a class of sixteen and the average age of my peers was forty-five, I was sometimes given the scenes for the pretty girls. They were offered to me as a promotion, which was lost on me, because I was much happier being considered perfect for the role of Karen as opposed to Grace on *Will and Grace*.

I was never great at the "pretty and safe" characters; give me the meaty, over-the-top, comic-relief characters anytime, as we all know no female character who is described as "sassy" and/or "bold" will ever be the title character (eye roll emoji).

I really loved being funny, and I seemed to be pretty good at it. Partially deaf family members always enjoyed my off-the-cuff sets at Christmas dinners, and my character-filled eulogies at pets' funerals always hit the spot.

But the fact that I didn't look like Rachel, Monica, or Phoebe, or have a penis like Jim Carrey, always seemed to get in the way. (SIDEBAR: I recently had a meeting with Mr. Tom Ford [WTF!!!!!!!], and he said I would have been a great Phoebe. We will be married in the fall.) If you're a woman and super funny but not super pretty, then you are deemed unsafe, hysterical, and full-on, and no number of Hail Marys will fix that.

When I hit drama school I had a massive brain fart and wanted people to see me as a serious actor, not just a funny, silly comedic actor. Comedy is my safe place (and as we know, I like safe, comfortable places, such as heated rain forests), so I thought because it wasn't a challenge enough for me, it wasn't a challenge for anyone and it wouldn't be respected.

Instead, I tried so hard to focus on serious roles. I performed Lady Macbeth's "Out, damned spot!" speech for my drama school audition, on which I was accepted, though I do believe I wasn't accepted into the school because I nailed the monologue, rather because I was brave enough to attempt it (pity uni acceptance emoji).

I studied at drama school for three years. Over that time, I lost my comedy spark. I struggled through the entire course because I wasn't interested in most of the roles I was playing. (Keep your eye out for my follow-up book, *Drama School: The Greatest Mindfuck of Them All*.)

It was a crazy, exhilarating time. There were anywhere between twenty and twenty-four of us in each other's faces, houses, beds, studios, ten hours a day, six days a week.

Drama school was a big fucked-up family dynamic that completely shaped my self-worth and also made me want to open a vein.

The One about Surviving Drama School

When I arrived at drama school, I had moved out of the house from the Gold Coast to Sydney at the age of seventeen and wasn't sure how I was going to survive.

I had auditioned for the Queensland University of Technology (QUT) and didn't get in. It was no surprise that I wasn't accepted, as this particular audition was held in Brisbane in November and I was balls deep into schoolies week. (Schoolies week, for those of you who are cultured and read books, is a week at the end of each year when graduating Year 12 students cut loose, and Surfers Paradise on the Gold Coast is the mecca for teenagers who can still fit into size 8 jeans and want to act like Prince Harry circa 2007–2012 but expect to be treated with the respect that one would show a heart surgeon. It's a shit fight, full of drunk teenagers crying, drinking, fighting, and crying some more. It's also a hub for Toolies—anyone older than the graduating age looking for child brides.)

I assured my mum that I'd be fine to audition AND attend a full week of drinking and debauchery at schoolies. A group of friends and I organized a hotel room, and most of our partying was held there. We only went out to Cavill Avenue once or twice to use our fake IDs and hopefully be on the news.

Mum picked me up on the morning of the audition from the shitty hotel we had rented. (Even though we only lived about half an hour from Surfers, we still felt it completely necessary to hire a room for the entire week, as it was imperative that we partook in a completely plastered and underwhelming week. It was the '90s, leave me alone.) When Mum arrived, I was awake and ready, not completely coherent, and still wearing last night's outfit, which Mum vetoed the moment she saw me. But I was awake and ready nonetheless.

When we arrived at the audition, I was terrible, didn't take direction, didn't remember any of my monologue, and I'm pretty sure when we were put into groups, every time I spoke, people took a polite step backward with their hands over their noses and mouths.

My audition for Theatre Nepean was completely different. I was ready. Ready to smash it. Ready to show what I had. And ready to not be yelled at by my mum again for being drunk and wasting her time.

It was a two-day audition process. Day one, we performed our prepared monologue in front of everyone, and if we managed to kick this in the dick, we were asked back the following day to do group workshops. On this first day of auditions, I met Ange and we became instant friends.

After getting accepted into the course, I inquired about deferring for a year because I had been offered a job to spend a summer abroad teaching drama at summer camps in America. Turns out, though, you can't defer a course that only accepts twenty-four students and carefully picks a specific group of people each year based on their ability and how they will mesh as a group.

So I kissed my dreams of summer camp goodbye and was relieved when Ange called to tell me that she had been accepted as well and that she had found a place for us to live, if I wanted to live with her. FUCK YES, I WANTED TO LIVE WITH THIS WOMAN! I moved to Penrith (Penrith is near Sydney, IT'S NOT SYDNEY, but it's near Sydney) and threw myself headlong into drama school.

I had Ange from the beginning, then met Kika and an army of other aspiring actor misfits. We were all in the same year together. Kika had the voice of an angel and, from the day I met her in the library and thought her name was Marika McFace, which made her cry laughing, I knew I was safe. And then I met Sipple. Sipple was my uni gay.

"Hi, I'm Celeste."

"I'm Sipple."

"Pardon?"

"Sipple."

"Like nipple?"

"Fuck you."

FRIENDSHIP!

I grabbed on to him and from that day on I never let him go. Drama school was full of antidepressants, bad Shakespeare monologues (mine), and weird passion speeches. But Sipple introduced me to JLo and loved cars like my dad so I was sticking with him. He loved to do high kicks and I loved to watch him, and for every one step he took I took three.

He was a serial monogamist and kept falling in love with straight guys, and straight girls kept falling in love with him. Another girl in our year claimed him as *her* gay, but Sipple and I know the truth: he was mine, forever. Whenever we would argue, I would always go up to him afterward and ask if we were OK, to which he would respond, "Argh!!! Of course we are. I love the fucking shit out of you."

We had the most ridiculous and geek-like fun together. We were studying in Penrith in Western Sydney, where it was either snowing or hotter than the sun, and Sipple and I would make the most of it. In winter, we would sit in the car with the air conditioner on as low as it could go and see who could last the longest; he would always win. And in summer, when it was so hot that the soap in our shower would melt, we would sit in the same car with the heater on as hot as possible. This wasn't as fun, and we later learned that there are ad campaigns against people being dickheads and doing something so stupid.

Sipple got me through drama school, and I love the fucking shit out of him for it.

A few things they don't tell you about drama school.

- If you cry, you pass. If you know famous people, you pass. You will not learn ANYTHING about the industry.

- You will learn everything there is to know about stitching a period costume and how to fit it on the same actress year after year.

- You will have sex with people who if you met later in life, you would report to the authorities.

- You think it will never end. EVER.

- Your classmates become your family; then you have sex with them and the end-of-year play gets weird.

- Everyone is gay for a minute.

- Everyone is tortured and misunderstood.

- Deodorant and toothpaste are kryptonite.

- If a lecturer gets cast in a show, then that class is canceled for the rest of the term.

Whatever you experience in your childhood, no matter how traumatic, will be brought up and you will be forced to deal with it while surrounded by nonprofessionals with bruised egos.

The One with Another Gross Man #timesup

When I graduated from drama school I was keen as mustard to work, and I hoped that I might end up with one of those stories where I say: "Oh, it was really weird. I was just eating an ice cream in a small ice cream shop and someone came up to me in that tiny little unassuming ice cream shop and said, 'Wow, you seem like you have amazing comic timing. I'd love to cast you in the next female-driven comedy film as well as make you head writer and regular cast member of *Saturday Night Live*.'" Turns out that can only happen to Natalie Portman, kind of.

I was excited by the prospect of work after graduating, as I had realized that I'm a nicer person when I'm acting and a better and richer person when I'm working as an actor.

Because work wasn't coming in as thick and fast as I'd hoped, I thought I would have to hustle to really get my own Natalie Portman story cracking. I decided I'd go through the paper and reply to one "actors wanted for shitty, soul-destroying gig" advertisement a week. Hustle!

One night, after spending the evening at my bestie Marika McFace's house eating all her ice cream and listening to her and her roommate, Rachel, talk about the awesome kids' theater companies they were going to open together, I was driving home and heard on the radio that a production company was looking for a funny girl in her midtwenties to audition for a new low-budget Aussie film.

For my non-Australian readers: "low-budget film" in Australia doesn't mean having to share a forty-foot trailer with your costar and only having a choice between Evian and fresh baby coconuts to rehydrate you after a full eight-hour day; it's more like bringing all the clothes you, your sister, your mum, and your weird old neighbor own and sharing them among the cast (which is usually just you and your friend, who is a trained vet but has been offered this job because she is happy to work for equity minimum) and making sure you've packed your iPhone charger, as the camera guy will need to charge up the camera every hour.

Well, holy shit, I didn't even need to look in the paper for the crappy job this week—the shitty job had come to me via my earholes and commercial radio. Look out, *Star Wars*, I'm on my way!

I pulled over to the side of the road and wrote down the number the overenthusiastic radio announcer had spat out at a million miles an hour. I called the station straightaway. You've got to get onto these things; *Bridesmaids 2* wasn't going to cast itself.

It was about 9:30 p.m., so the phone lines weren't busy, and I got through and spoke to the station producer off air. I inquired about the job, and of course they didn't know too much about it, as the announcer had just been reading a brief that had been sent in by the film producer's assistant.

I gave the guy my number, and he gave me the contact details of the production company. Yes! I'm in business. I continued driving home and did a quick vocal warm-up on the way, as I wanted my voice to be all warm and Cate Blanchett–like when I spoke to the film producer, who I would no doubt be thanking in my Oscars speech when I won for Best Actor in a Foreign Film the following year.

Before I even got home, my phone rang. It was a private number and I thought this was it—they were calling to offer me the role and I didn't even need to audition.

I pulled over again and did one last tongue stretch and vocal trill before answering the phone.

To my surprise, it wasn't the producer from the film or the producer from the radio station I had just called; rather, it was the station DJ. The dude who had just been talking a million miles an hour. I was kind of puzzled but was happy to take the call.

He was calling to see if I had called the film company yet and just to warn me to be careful, as they (the radio station) had no idea about the film or the production company or anything at all connected with them, so he just wanted to cover his and his employer's arses. Fair enough.

We got to talking, and he said I had a great sense of humor (he's only human, I guess) and I'd be great on radio. He asked if I wanted to come into the station the following night and do an interview about being an aspiring actor.

Um, sure, why not. It might not be my Natalie Portman story, but Harrison Ford was a carpenter on a film before he became a Harrison Ford, so I thought I might be able to do something similar via radio.

I was excited. I had a new focus: I was going to dominate the airwaves, much like Janet Jackson dominated my teenage years.

I went into the radio station the following night at eight o'clock and was super excited. Radio! Of course, I was always told I would be good on radio—but I was also told that getting a spiral perm was a good thing, so you know, grain of salt.

When I got there, I had to call at the front desk, who then called reception, who called security to come and collect me. We walked through a series of glass doors that only a special swipe card could activate. After we went through what felt like four hundred doors in silence,

I was expecting Ryan Seacrest to be at the end of the soundproof tunnel, or at the very least Harry Potter.

When I was swiped into the radio booth, I was greeted by a very over-the-top guy who had a fantastic face for radio. He waved for me to sit down in a fancy bouncy chair, and a thirteen-year-old assistant who was far too cheery for any time of the day told me how to use the headphones and microphone. (For the record, you just put the headphones on your head and talk into the microphone; it's really not rocket science. Fuck, if Kyle Sandilands can do it, any monkey with a brain injury can.)

About an hour went by while we bantered on and off air with people coming in and out of the studio; then around 9:00 p.m. everyone clocked off—everyone except me and the DJ. His shift ended at 10:00 p.m. He said I was doing really well and that he would love to get me in once a week for an hour to have a chat, as I had a natural talent for radio. Awesome!

After everyone left, the conversation took a turn. He started asking me questions about sex—what I liked about it and how often I had it. I felt a bit weird, but I kind of let it go when he turned it into a segment and we got listeners to call in and talk about their sex lives. I heard a commercial radio station once got a woman to wet herself on air to win some cash, and given the late time slot, the discussion didn't seem too out of place. And I was twenty and had never done this thing before, so who was I to say what was and wasn't acceptable on late-night commercial radio?

I asked the DJ what happened overnight at the radio station. Did someone come in and do the graveyard shift? Was it prerecorded? If so, what time did the next show kick off?

He told me that from 10:00 p.m. to 5:00 a.m. the station ran itself; he needed to press a few buttons at the end of his show and then it would run smoothly until the next person came in the following morning.

I love a bit of behind-the-scenes. I always look for those bits on a DVD. I was intrigued; this was all super fancy and exciting. I was like a sponge (one of the good-quality, expensive ones), and I couldn't get enough.

He told me that he had once forgotten to program the overnight prerecorded shows and had got as far as his car and realized that the station had been silent for about half an hour, so he panicked and ran back up through all the secure swipe doors and pressed the buttons.

Oh, how we laughed. "How crazy!" I said. "Did you get in trouble?"

"No, of course not," he said.

Toward the end of the shift, after almost two hours in the studio, I had to use the bathroom. He said he needed to swipe me into the bathroom, because this place was not only broadcasting commercial pop music but obviously also housing all of Kris Kardashians embryos; this was the only possible explanation for the ridiculous number of locks, codes, and swipe cards.

I believed him—why wouldn't I? I mean, I needed to be swiped in everywhere else by a man, so why wouldn't a man swipe me into the bathroom? When I asked if I could just take the card and go on my own, he said it didn't work like that and that he wasn't allowed to let anyone swipe his card but him.

He "threw to a song" (which is just wanker shop talk for pressed "Play") and escorted me to the bathroom.

When we reached the women's toilet, he swiped me in and placed his hand on my lower back to usher me through.

Gross. I rushed through with a little gallop to dislodge his spindly fingers from me and hurried into the nearest stall.

As I tried to close the stall door behind me, I realized there was something preventing me from closing and locking it. I turned around and saw that not only had he swiped me into the toilets; he had also followed me in and was standing with his arm atop the stall door, holding it open.

I froze.

"Um, what are you doing?"

"You know what I'm doing."

"Can you get out, please? I need to pee."

"That's OK, I'll help you."

"Are you fucking kidding?"

He reached down to my skirt and tried to lift it up.

I hit his hand away. "Fuck off! I don't need your help." As I tried to push him out, he pushed back.

"Oh fuck!" I thought. "I'm alone in Fort Knox with a man twice my size who is pushing himself onto me in a bathroom stall. FUCK FUCK FUCK FUCK FUCK."

I pushed harder and finally managed to push him out and close the stall door. Thank God—not any god in particular at this point, just anyone that was available and listening.

He laughed and stood on the other side of the door and waited for me. He just stood there and waited. I could see his ugly shoes under the toilet door.

"You don't need to wait."

"Yes, I do. I need to swipe you back into the studio." Fuck.

I froze, again. So did my kidneys.

I sat on the toilet with the seat down and pulled out my phone, thinking if I could call or text anyone, then I'd be sweet. I'd call Marika, stay on the phone with her the whole time while I got out of the stall, the toilet, and the radio station; then I'd send up a fucking flare as soon as I got outside and stand aside as the SWAT team moved in to take this prick down while I called his mother, alerting her to what a disappointment he is.

But of course there wasn't any phone reception in this radio station from hell.

I got up from the toilet seat and slowly opened the stall door, and he was standing at the basin directly in front of me. Just staring at me. I walked to a basin farther away and he followed. He stood behind me and looked at me in the mirror. He was standing so close I could feel his breath on my neck.

I kept my head down and focused on washing my hands. I cleaned them so well that I could have performed open-heart surgery. He didn't move or take his eyes off me. Fuck.

As I moved past him he grabbed my arm, trying to pull me back to him. I snatched my arm back and stared at his stupid man face.

"You really need to stop doing that."

He smiled at me with mean eyes as I walked toward the bathroom door, planning on kicking the fucking thing in.

I pushed on the door and it opened! The stupid security swipe-arse door opened! NO DUMB SWIPEY CARD NEEDED!

I walked to the next door, with him right behind me, and pushed on it too, except *this* dumb door needed to be swiped.

Again I froze. I just stared at the door with my head down. Praying the powers of Eleven from *Stranger Things* would be gifted to me in that moment and I could blow that fucking door off its hinges.

He walked up behind me again, and I could feel his body against mine.

I couldn't move. I was pinned between this predator man and the dumb-arse door. Trapped.

He leaned forward and slowly reached across my body to swipe the door open. The door beeped and I pushed it and ran to the next door as he slowly walked up behind me and repeated this game of fuckwit and mouse.

This continued for about three more doors and what felt like the rest of my twenties. When I finally got back to the studio, I grabbed my bag and without looking at him said, "I'm going now. Can you please swipe me out?"

He sat down at his desk, put his headphones on, and said, "I'll just call security to come and get you, or do you want me to personally swipe you out?"

"Security."

I stood outside the studio door and waited for the security guard to come and get me. When he arrived I ran to him much like Blac Chyna ran to get a pregnancy test when she knew she was carrying a Kardashian baby: with desperation and relief.

I must have looked pretty shaken up, because the kind security guard—who didn't follow me into a bathroom stall, who didn't breathe down my neck, who didn't try to take my skirt off or press himself up against me—asked if I was OK.

"Yep, I'm fine." I dismissed it and just wanted to get into my car.

My dad has always told me that once you get into the car, just go, day or night. Don't stuff around and check your phone or do anything—just get in, lock the door, put your seat belt on, and drive. I'm a good Catholic girl, so I always do what I'm told. I got into my car and got the hell out of there.

When I pulled up at the first set of lights, I checked my phone. (Don't message me about being on my phone in the car—I was freaking out! I had just been harassed by a pimply-faced pig. Let's all just stay focused please?!)

There was one message on my phone. It was from him. Hey, it's really cold outside, do you want me to come and keep you warm?

I texted back immediately. I didn't even think about it. No. Fuck off.

My phone beeped almost immediately. It was him. AGAIN. Don't come back in next week.

And that was that. I didn't let him fuck me in the toilet, so I wasn't welcome back into the studio, and the side window that I had hoped to use to access my hopes and dreams because the front door was always closed now also seemed jammed shut.

Even in the telling of this story (and the story about the Big Fat Talentless Old Man at Jupiter's Casino), I have realized that women need to be careful. It's so common for it to seem as if we are telling our stories to defame men or profit from the stories financially, because God forbid that women would just want to be heard. *Not* naming the perpetrators shows that it's not just individuals to blame but a sick culture that needs to be disarmed.

And just for the record, I don't give two shits about what these stories do to certain men's careers or reputations, especially if they are lucky enough to *have* a career that they didn't have to fuck someone to get.

For so long women have had to put up with a strong culture of intimidation, threats, and men just being fucking gross.

But not anymore.

#timesup.

The One about Sparky

I graduated from drama school in 2002, and after a few years of performing in a number of not-for-profit plays I landed a role on the Australian medical drama *All Saints* in 2005.

A Brief History of Australian TV

In early-2000s Australia, we basically made four drama shows a year: *Neighbours*, *Home and Away*, *Blue Heelers*, and *All Saints*.

Neighbours and *Home and Away* are our staple soap operas, which we call "dramas." The casts are made up of a handful of seasoned performers with mortgages to pay, a heap of bikini models, former *Bachelorette* and *Australian Idol* contestants, and OCCASIONALLY a random Hemsworth. If you are lucky enough to secure a job on either of these shows, you can then expect to move to America and become a movie star, all the while thanking the tiny Australian industry for telling you that you are beautiful and hiring you because of it.

Neighbours and *Home and Away* have been on the air for thirty-three and thirty years, respectively, and only once in a blue moon will they kill off a character, revive them, kill them off again, bring them back as an evil twin, then finally kill them off once and for all to make room for a new cast member named Margot Robbie or Tiffany McYoga Face. This leaves little opportunity for actors in Australia who don't identify as swimsuit models to practice their craft and work in their chosen field.

When you tell people you are an actor in Australia, the first question you get asked is "What have you been in?" and the second question is "Have you been in *Home and Away*?" To which I would answer (respectively) "None of your business" and "Yes."

Blue Heelers was a police drama that was on air for thirteen years and was great for actors in the Australian TV industry who *didn't* look like Victoria's Secret models but wanted to get some exposure on TV. Aside from the core cast of police officers, each week saw a new group of characters come and go on the show: criminals, victims, local shop owners, and a random dog. It was great: a heap of talented actors and a ton of shit ones got to sink their teeth into scripts playing the pivotal characters for that week's episode, allowing them to hold their heads high that Christmas when annoying aunties would ask if they had done any real acting yet.

The situation was similar on *All Saints*, Australia's longest-running medical drama. (I like to think of it as *Grey's Anatomy* meets *ER*, only George Clooney and McDreamy forgot to show up for their shifts.)

The setting of the show originated in Ward 17, where a core cast of doctors and nurses pretended not to want to have sex with each other. Then it moved to the emergency room, opening up the possibility for a lot more guest roles and semiregular gigs for us actors.

And this is where I met the late, great Mark Priestley.

In 2004, I was working at a really shitty dress shop in Balmain. (Not the European brand, pronounced *bol-moin*; rather a suburb in the Inner West of Sydney that housed fancy restaurants, excellent coffee, and a bevy of awesome, charismatic homeless men. Two of my favorites were DJ Darling Street and Michael, a gentleman who always wore a suit soiled with urine [his own], slept out in front of the police station, and at least once a week would walk down the main street of Balmain waving around a wad of fifty-dollar notes and shouting, "Yep, that's fucking right, mah bitches," to the tune of Elvis's "Blue Suede Shoes.")

Balmain was awesome. It's the first place #hothusband and I lived together. Our house was small and didn't really have a floor; there was carpet, but there wasn't much under it.

We loved it there. On New Year's Eve the place was sectioned off because the main street led down to the harbor and uninterrupted views of the Harbour Bridge, where at midnight millions of dollars' worth of fireworks would light up the city. So Balmain was a sought-after location on NYE. The only way in or out was to show the traffic controller your ID and address.

It was a magical suburb that you never had to leave, so when I scored a job at the local shitty clothing store I was stoked.

After working in the clothing store for six months, I got an audition for *All Saints* as paramedic Bree Matthews. My audition consisted of dramatic looks off camera and made-up medical jargon. It was a guest role, just one episode, and I nailed it.

I fleshed it out to a four-year, semiregular gig. Not because I'm a magical unicorn actor who can turn dust into an Oscars speech (we all know that only Marion Cotillard can do that), but because I can hustle.

I really respect the Hustle. I believe Madonna to be the originator. She's not a great singer or dancer, but that hustler deserves a Nobel Prize for her services to the Hustle. She has turned it into a career. Think Lisa Rinna—her Hustle has become about talking about what a hustler she is. Respect.

I worked that *All Saints* set and my professional relationships much like Britney works an Auto-Tune. And I succeeded, continuing to make up medical jargon alongside some of my most favorite actors. I was finally contracted as a main character six weeks before the show was canceled (red frustrated face emoji).

Mark played nurse Dan Goldman. I don't remember the first time I met him, as I don't really remember a time without him in my life. He got me. He knew what I was capable of as an actor before *I* even knew it. We would fuck around on set all the time, doing everything we could to put each other off. I was always worried I was going to get fired, but he never cared if it pissed people off. No one would ever fire Mark, because he was Mark, a creative genius who would throw a pencil in your face five seconds before the director called action, then as soon as the camera rolled he would lovingly kiss an elderly character on the forehead and say his final goodbye, having everyone in tears and unable to move on to the next scene.

He was a comic genius and made me feel like I was one too. At one stage during my stint on *All Saints* I was performing in a low-budget, not-for-profit theater show, *BoyBand*, in which I played the band's choreographer. (Did I mention I used to dance?) The show was a comical look at what goes on behind the scenes of an overproduced, overmanaged boy band. (We thought we were geniuses: we changed the lyrics of a Backstreet Boys song from "Backstreets back, all right" to "I suck cock, all night"; there were some really top-shelf gags.)

Mark and I had worked on a few episodes of *All Saints* together and weren't super-close friends at this stage, but I fucking loved him and was a little starstruck by him and was completely beside myself when he came to a performance of *BoyBand*.

After the show I went up to him and asked what he thought. (NB I fucking hate going to the foyer after a show; it is my least favorite thing to do—well, that and putting petrol in my car. Everyone, and I mean EVERYONE, is a dickhead in the after-show foyer; no one looks you in the eye, everyone becomes a contestant on *RuPaul's Drag Race*, claiming everything you did was a fucking revelation, and people you've never met before feel it's OK to kiss you hard on the mouth. I, too, am one of these dickhead people. Something comes over me, I feel I can't look anyone in the eye, and I'm sure it seems as though I'm looking over your shoulder for someone more exciting to talk to when in actual fact I *am* looking over your shoulder, only because I'm trying to find the nearest exit, or more to the point wondering when the hell the catering is going to bring the plate of spring rolls to me first, as requested.)

Mark was with some mutual friends and we were chatting, and with a stomach full of cheap white wine the color of a UTI I asked him the dreaded question you must ask when in a foyer: "So did you like it?"

To which he responded, "Not really."

Right. Good. Yep, I like honesty, and Mark was the Godfather of honesty.

I also become a glutton for punishment in these hellish foyers, trying to prove that I'm down to earth and really open to suggestions and criticism (which no actor wants ever; I don't care how hard we try to convince you that we want your honest feedback, DON'T FUCKING DO IT, it's a trap, you will be bitched about in dressing rooms and shared green rooms for the rest of time).

Me: So not even the lyrics that we changed from the Backstreet Boys song "As Long as You Love Me" to "As Long as You Fuck Me"?

Mark: No. Not really.

(Silence. Where the hell are those spring rolls?)

Mark: You were awesome.

Me: Pardon?

Mark: The show was really bad, but you were great. You're really funny and have great comic timing.

Me: Shut up!

Mark: What?

Me: I'm not great with compliments.

Mark: I can tell.

And that was that. We spent time with each other at work after that and became best friends for life.

I loved working with him. He challenged me and scared me, he put me strongly in my comfort zone and then would fuck with me, and it was the best. He taught me to leave pages of my script all around set and attach them to the set and props (e.g., medical charts, underneath beds), and because we worked on a medical drama and the scripts were so full of medical-speak, I learned to just read the lines from the secret stash of scripts or disguise it as reading someone's medical history.

He would come over to my place in Balmain in the middle of the night with a dodgy movie camera in his cross-body bag and a shit-eating grin on his face, wanting to shoot something, anything, and I couldn't resist. We would write and shoot stuff all night, and it was awesome. As we wrote we would laugh at each other and couldn't get enough of it. We didn't need an audience; we just loved making each other laugh.

He is the main person in my life who made me realize that not only was I funny, but I also had an understanding of comedy that could take me really far. He gave me space as a comedian. He thought I was great, and he will never know how great I really thought *he* was.

In TV Land there is a lot of waiting around; I'm pretty sure *War and Peace* was written in between scenes on the set of *The Golden Girls*.

The downtime—the time when people would go over their lines, go to the bathroom, carry on affairs in dressing rooms—was when Mark and I would get busy. We would play around with ideas to prepare for him coming over to my house and filming that night. I doubted myself a lot, and it would annoy him.

Me: I don't really know if that's funny.

Mark: You're being boring.

Me: What do you mean?

Mark: I don't know why you do this. It's really boring.

Me: What?

Mark: Doubting yourself. You're really funny and know exactly what you're doing.

Me: Thanks.

Mark: So can you just stop it? It's really fucking annoying.

Mark changed everything for me. He was my best friend, and him not being around anymore is a big bag of not-so-funny comedy dicks. I loved him so much as an actor and a fully qualified dickhead. I would just be in awe of his love and aggressive support of me.

When Mark got sick it broke me. I saw his dark thoughts come in and surround him and make him sicker and sicker, but I didn't focus too much on it because he said he was fine, so he was fine.

Api had to move out of our Balmain palace to take care of his daughters full-time, so I had a spare room, and Mark asked if he could move in. I said no. I worried that it would have been too full-on and I wouldn't have been able to handle it. I said I had someone else moving in, which was a big fat lie.

Truth is, I wish I'd been honest with him. If I'd told him I was worried about living with him, he would have been fine with it, because he loved me. I mean, he would have yelled at me first and called me an idiot, but he would have been fine. He understood himself and his impact on others more than anyone, and I wish more than anything I hadn't lied to him six weeks before he killed himself. I should have been a better friend to him. It wouldn't have saved him; he just would have known how much I loved him when he died.

Mark had the fragility and wit of Jim Carrey. Which makes my heart sing. And I hold on to this when I unintentionally stumble on *The Big Bang Theory* in a stoner's haze and think comedy is dead.

The One about Thomas

I fell in love with my gay best friend in a way that one would see only in a Shakespearean play or on *Will and Grace* (the old episodes—the reboot is too predictable).

I had seen him on a documentary about what it's like to study acting at the National Institute of Dramatic Art (NIDA). A film crew would follow him and three other first-year acting students around, asking them about their "process." All the actors featured had something unique: one was loud, one was pretty but annoying, and Thomas was an amazing character actor who happened to be born without a left hand. So in classic drama school style they completely exploited him and filmed him as he went into prosthetic hand appointments that were organized and paid for by the drama school—so they happily informed the viewer.

We met at a call center: an obvious place to set a love story. The first time I saw him I yelled across the room, "I know you!" He was shocked and startled and scared that he was in trouble. Traits that over our subsequent fifteen-year friendship I have realized are his go-to emotional states.

We hit it off straightaway. I was overbearing and charming as hell, which is what I do when I meet someone I like and want to show them that I'm cool and they can be themselves around me, when really I'm dying inside, wishing I'd stayed at home and cried myself to sleep.

He was funny, kind, bitchy, smart, talented, and insecure: everything I was looking for in a gay husband. Only I didn't know he was gay! I thought I had finally met the bestest man ever and we were going to have babies together, or just adopt dogs; either situation I was happy with so long as it was with him.

I was so sad when I heard he was gay that I thought bitching about him to a mutual friend was the obvious thing to do.

Me: Um, do you know that Thomas is gay?

Friend: Are you serious?

Me: Yep.

Friend: Wow!

Me: I know, I couldn't believe it either. I was sure he was flirting with me.

Friend: Oh my God!

Me: It's kind of a shock, right?

Friend: Um, no! I can't believe you didn't know. He is so gay.

Me: What?!

Friend: Not only is Thomas gay, but he has been voted the gayest man in the world by all the gays.

Me: Fuck.

After getting over the heartbreak that he would never fully choose me in the way I wanted him to, I got so excited for our future together: Thomas and Celeste, the gay and the former child dancer! I fell deeply in love with him in a much more practical way, and we've been family ever since. We have written bad sitcoms together, he's the godfather to my children, he's in my favorites call list, above my manager but below my husband (of course).

In 2007, Thomas and I decided to travel around America together for a month, and we still talk about every element of the trip to this day. I was excited for America to meet us as a duo. It was one of the greatest and most traumatic experiences of my life.

We neglected to discuss our hopes and dreams for the overpriced trip, which started with us arguing about who got the aisle seat on the 6,738-hour flight over. And our first day in the States was highlighted by Thomas checking in to our accommodation, kissing me on the cheek, and heading to his first midday orgy.

One night in New York we went to an excellent gay club, where no one looked like they "should," everyone used whatever toilet they wanted, and Thomas told me after enjoying fourteen free-pour vodkas that if he weren't gay he would marry me (salsa dancing plus heartbreak emoji).[6]

We saw the Rockettes do all the jazz steps in the world. Thomas is a musical theater FREAK, so he was determined to see every goddamned show that had ever been mounted, remounted, made into a movie, recast, then remounted again while we were in New York. I was more about walking along Fifth Avenue pointing at all the tiny dogs and lollypop ladies with big hair.

On Christmas Eve, we went to a club with musicals playing on the big screen. It was a Monday, and they named it "Musical Mondays."

---

6   Dear America, your current president is an arse-hankie and your gun-control laws (or lack thereof) are bullshit, but well done on the free pours. They really are one of the only things that keep us coming back—well, that and Erika Jayne.

(See what they did there?) We sang all the show tunes in the world, Thomas flirted, and I was the BEST wingwoman ever. Every time things started heating up, I would take myself to the bar and buy drinks, only to return to Thomas standing alone asking me where the hell I had gone. After a solid four hours of singing out of key, I wanted to go home with my best friend Thomas, looking at Christmas lights on the way and just generally making festive memories. Instead, Thomas walked me out the front, got my jacket on the way, called a cab, put me in it, and waltzed back into the club ready to open up shop.

We had planned the trip so that we were in New York for Christmas and got the fuck out of there on New Year's Eve to bring in the New Year in Vegas. Thomas decided *I* would organize and pay for Christmas activities and *he* would organize and pay for NYE debauchery.

So I booked a restaurant in NYC after seeing it on an episode of *Sex and the City* (hello, child of consumerism!). We went with two other friends who were in New York at the time: Mark and Kate.

SIDEBAR: As you already know, Mark was one of my closest friends and greatest supporters. He made me laugh and challenged me every day we spent together up until his death in 2008.

Kate Mulvany is by far the most gracious, kind, and inspiring person in my life. If I'm doing a show and I know she's in the audience, I look forward to her after-show text (which she ALWAYS sends) nearly as much as I look forward to my postshow wine. She is one of the greatest playwrights the world has seen, and I thank Mark every day that he brought her into my life.

Now, I love Mark and Kate a whole bunch, but nothing accelerates a friendship like seeing your mates on the other side of the world while it's bloody cold, the Macy's Christmas windows are in full flight, and you're about five beers deep.

All four of us lost our minds when we met up on the corner of Let's Get Drunk in NYC Avenue and West FUCK YEAH! Street. We jumped and screamed and couldn't get to the Christmas dinner I had organized quick enough.

Charlotte (me), Samantha (Thomas), Miranda (Mark), and Carrie (Kate) all made our way uptown to the super-chic, super-fabulous *SATC* restaurant ready to make some serious memories. Turns out you can't believe everything you see on TV! I know, right—WHAT?! The food was overpriced and undercooked and could have fit in the palm of Trump's tiny little stupid hand.[7]

The four of us sat and pretended to eat for the assigned twenty-three minutes we were allowed to be there, drank, pushed our full servings of crumbs around our expensive plates, drank, then left. We went to a local diner and ate burgers and fries until 3:00 a.m., when we decided to go on a horse-and-carriage ride around Central Park, where Mulvany thought she had found her long-lost Irish uncle, Thomas and I continued to argue, and Mark filmed it. All. Of. It.

Then Thomas and I left Mark and Kate in New York and headed to Vegas for New Year's Eve, and it was Thomas's turn to underfeed us for a hearty fee. Only he totally stepped up: he had arranged for us to go to TAO Nightclub for a party that was being hosted by the one and only Mariah "Don't Light Me from Above" Carey. It was free drinks and sushi for the first two hours; then we had to pay after that.

So in classic Thomas fashion, we got there as soon as the doors opened at 6:00 p.m. and decided that he would stand in the drinks line and I would stand in the sushi line (he also loves a plan), and we drank and drank and drank and ate and drank for the first two hours like our lives depended on it.

By the time Mariah came out at 11:59:55 p.m., I couldn't feel my knees, and Thomas was so excited that he started crying tears of vodka. Mariah was on a platform above the crowd (obviously), pretending to sing something, and everyone had their hands up screaming her

---

7   Sorry for saying the T word.

name—well, everyone except Thomas, as his 453,920 drinks had kicked in and he was the only person facing the back wall wondering what all the noise was and screaming "WHERE THE FUCK IS SHE?!"

Our American trip came at a time when we wanted different things. Thomas was always wanting to be out meeting with the boys, while I wanted to skip around the city hand in hand singing "New York, New York." This wasn't a recipe for the best time. But there is no one else in the world I could travel with, fight with, and still want to share a platonic bed with.

Thomas is my most bestest friend. I do have to share him with other ladies as well, and that's fine, but he's mine. Whenever I am in the city for work I stay with him. He calls me wife (along with his other ladies), and we share a bed when I'm there. He is one of the greatest actors and always makes me want to be better and braver in my work.

I have vowed to love him forever and never go overseas with him ever again.

That was, until we got drunk and booked our next trip.

We are about to embark on a three-month tour around America. Be sure to buy Thomas's follow-up book, *She's Not that Funny in Real Life*, to see if we survived.

The One about My Love for the LGBTQI Community

Dear gays,

I'm sorry, I'm really sorry that you are treated the way you are. It's a bag of dicks, and not in the good way you and I wish it was.

Australia recently had a $122 million plebiscite to determine whether you should have the right to marry. I can confirm three things: I have no idea of the definition of a "plebiscite," I don't even know how much $122 million is, and this is all a big sack of shit. For some reason our dumb and embarrassing government thinks that us straighty-180s should be able to vote on what rights you excellent gay folk are allowed to have.

For the record, I voted a resounding YES. A big, fat "fuck yes," and I'm proud that most people that I surround myself with—aside from the odd homophobic second-removed cousin from my husband's side of the family proclaiming "it's Adam and Eve, not Adam and Steve"; after a few wines and many attempts from my husband to keep me away from him I yelled, "It can be Eve and fucking Maude if it wants to be!" (not my finest hour)—did the same. We are all loud and proud and gay on your behalf.

I have always felt so loved and supported by the LGBTQI community; you guys and gals allowed me to be loud and confronting and all the while helped me with my posture and eyeliner. From being the love interest of a number of lesbians (a career highlight, if I'm going to be honest) to sharing a bed and cuddle with my gay boys because they got me more than anyone else, I never felt like I needed to be something else when around you.

I voted Yes! YES! because equality, YES! because love, and YES! because YASS! I bought equality stickers to put on my car and computer, and I called everyone I knew to make sure they would do the same, and I've been watching *Brokeback Mountain* and *Priscilla, Queen of the Desert* on a loop in support.

There were a lot of campaigns supporting the no vote (and there still are, even though they lost!), and for an unwarranted reason I took much offense to these bullshit campaigns. There were ads on TV featuring "concerned mothers" with bad hair and what looked like a prickly stick up their arse saying that if "we" allowed gay couples to marry, then there would be more same-sex role-playing in schools. I wish! I would LOVE my boys to be taught about equal rights as opposed to the bigoted bullshit that gets shoved down kids' throats.

There were skywriters simply writing the words "Vote No" over Sydney. This was done by the same company that wrote "Trump" in skywriting during the pro-women marches,[8] so it just seemed like a rich dickhead who wasn't getting enough attention at home wanting to cause some harm with his plane.

I'm sorry for this. You deserve a lot more, especially as you have given so many of us weird, dramatic straight kids such confidence and support and valuable advice on what a nip and tuck can really achieve over the years.

I love you. I'm with you.

C x

---

8   Sorry.

The One with #hothusband

I have had only three serious boyfriends in my life, and I married one of them. I'm one of those annoying people who knew I was going to marry my husband as soon as I met him.

#sorrynotsorry.

My first boyfriend was when I was in Year 7, and he was excellent. We were so into each other, we were the It Couple of the year (well, that's what I tell my husband if we have a fight and I'm trying to make him jealous; I'm pretty sure no one else in the school even knew we were together). He was so passionate for a thirteen-year-old. He would sing all the lyrics of Boyz II Men "I Swear" and bought me the single "The Most Beautiful Girl in the World." He even wrote my sister a letter about how lucky she was to be related to me. He's only human. We planned our wedding: we would have all our family sitting on one side of the aisle and all our friends sitting on the other side, and as soon as the clock struck midnight, we would ditch the family and hit the clubs with our mates, because we were crazy yet considerate.

I lost my virginity at seventeen with my second serious boyfriend, who had as much hair on his back as he did his head. He was a footballer and a super-sensitive soul. He would cry if we had a fight and cry just as much if I told him I didn't like parsley. We were together for three emotional years but never planned our wedding.

I was the wingwoman at school. The go-between.

Year 9

Guy: Hey, Barber, can you go and ask Karen if she wants to sit with me on the way to the bird sanctuary?

Me: I thought we were going to sit together. I've got a heap of new gags I'm working on.

Guy: Nah, not today, mate. I want to feel Karen up on the way.

Me: Sweet! I so didn't want to sit next to you on that dumb bus anyway.

Guy: Oh, and ask her if she wants me to spit my gum out before we pash this time. [Pash is Australian for "make out." Let me put it in a sentence: "I totally pashed Tom Ford." I hope that clears it up for you.]

Me: Yep, of course I will ask her that; that seems like an awesome and considerate question. FYI, if I was pashing a guy like you, I would totally be fine with you doing whatever you want with your gum.

Guy: What?

Me: What?

At first I was totally cool with this role. I knew my place, I knew my worth, and I knew my sexual appeal, and I was very happy with all of it. Until I wasn't.

Year 10

Me: Um, can you start getting someone else to ask her this stuff? I feel weird doing it.

Guy: Why?

Me: I don't know, maybe I don't want to be your go-between girl anymore.

Guy: What are you talking about?

Me: Well . . .

Guy: You're not my go-between girl.

Me: Thanks.

Guy: You're like a brother to me.

Me: Awesome.

When guys started paying attention to me, it was a whole other level. It took a while. I like to wear people down over years with my subtle sexuality. And anyway, going from average brother-type friend to pageant beauty overnight can only happen to one girl per school, and Kimberly Hardcastle was the queen on that throne. Seriously, she went home one day with her nondescript mousy-brown hair and came back the next morning with platinum-blonde locks and a fringe that you could surf under, and her boobs did everything mine wouldn't—they pointed forward. It truly was an awakening for all of us. Well done, Kimberly.

If a guy was into me, it wasn't an overnight thing. He wouldn't wake up one morning and think, "Shit, Celeste! Oh God, it's always been Celeste, she has been in front of me this whole time and I didn't even realize. Wow, the way her monobrow joins in an unintimidating way, the way her double cowlicks really accentuate her small mouth—this is everything I've wanted when taking a lover." No, those weren't *my* teenage experiences.

When guys started paying attention to me, I didn't know how to behave or what it really meant. I thought that playing hard to get was the answer, as I saw pretty bikini models do that and I figured I'd follow suit. Turns out that the way pretty girls teased surfer boys was fun and flirtatious.

Surfer Boy: Hey, wanna go to the beach this arvo after school? ["Arvo" is horny surfer-speak for "afternoon."]

Pretty Girl: Um, I'm not sure. I think Cindi and I are going bikini shopping.

SB: Oh, sweet, I'll come and help you try on the swimmers if you want?

PG: Why would I want that? (Cute giggle, flicks hair.)

SB: You want an honest opinion, right?

PG: Well, I'm just going to go with Cindi and I might meet you at the beach later, and you can give me your opinion then.

Done, afternoon sorted.

When *I* would offer up my idea of flirtatious hard-to-get banter, it wasn't received so well.

Year 12

Surfer Boy: Oi, Barber, can I get a lift to the beach?

Me: Fuck yeah. I just have to sort out my tampon first.

SB: That's gross.

Me: Gross or kind of kinky? (Flicks hair, which is caught in mouth.)

SB: No, it's just fucking gross.

Me: Well, if you wanted to give me a hand with it, I could change your mind.

SB: Jesus, Barber, what's wrong with you?

Me: Want to watch me try on bikinis?

SB: You're weirding me out.

Me: Sorry, I'll just wear a pad.

This all changed when I met my husband. I went from Liz Lemon to Amber Rose in only ten short years.

I met #hothusband fifteen years ago. I was twenty-one and working at Dick's Hotel in Balmain and living in Kings Cross.

I had the greatest studio apartment in the Cross. It was big enough for a bedroom, a lounge room, and a dining area. If I'd put a wall up, it would have been a good-size one-bedroom apartment, and it was $115 a week, motherfuckers! That's how much I pay to park at Bondi Beach for two hours these days.

It was the best. I loved to just sit on my green velvet couch and watch *Friends* on my microwave-size TV while listening to junkies outside my window complain about the price of ice cream.

Dick's was on the other side of the city from where I lived. I'd get there around 3:00 p.m. for my 3:30 p.m. shift. I liked getting there early, as the kitchen usually had food left over from the lunch service, and I would help them with the scraps; I have always been charitable like that.

I mainly did night shifts, but on this day I had decided to do the double shift. And thank God I did.

Api walked in around lunchtime, and as soon as I saw him I couldn't take my eyes off him. Holy shit, he was beautiful. HOLY SHIT.

We looked at each other and smiled, and all the feelings that I experienced while watching *Wild Things* alone in my studio, I was feeling in that moment in that pub.

I was in the middle of pouring Trevor the local drunkard's beer (a half pint of Carlton that was $3.50 and Trevor would always, ALWAYS complain that I didn't give him enough change from the $3.20 he gave me. Fuck, Trevor! Get your life together!) when *he* walked in.

Api was wearing head-to-toe cheesecloth and had dreadlocks in a perfect Posh Spice bob circa 1998, and his smile—Jesus, that bloody smile—with his perfect teeth and his stupid sparkly eyes, I knew I was screwed. Well, fingers crossed. He smiled at me again, and I threw Trevor's half-poured beer at him with a "don't fuck this up for me, mate" look and got busy.

Api's cousin Craig was a local and would come into the pub most afternoons after work. He was dating one of the other girls who worked there and was always a good laugh.

Dick's was an old workers' pub and really lived up to its name (a name that I had embroidered across my breasts). The majority of the clientele were over Trevor's age and would be drinking in the pub when we opened at 10:00 a.m. They would leave only when their wives or children called looking for them, around dinnertime (sad face emoji).

So Craig was a welcome relief; he was fun and had an awesome sense of humor, and we got along well.

The weekend I met Api, he and Craig were on a bender. Just to clarify: he wasn't on a big night out with the boys or just having hair of the dog to get through the next day. No, he was on a full-blown bender. And after seeing Api, my main aim in life was to get caught up in the bending.

So it was on. I flirted with this Maori Adonis like it was my job and my Rent. Was. Due.

Every time the staff had to collect empty beer glasses from the tables—a job people hated doing—I would put my hand up to do it. Any excuse to be close to him, flirt with him, brush up against him, prevent him from stumbling over, I'd take it.

Turns out I wasn't the only one wanting a piece of this hot magical unicorn.

I was twenty-one and had a fight on my hands, as there was a group of women *a lot* older than me, around thirty-six, with my prey in their sights. One of them came up to me at the bar, ordered a vodka, and said through clenched teeth: "Step off, little one, this one's mine." I felt bad for them: they were at an old workers' pub looking for husbands, and as soon as Api walked in it was fucking hunting season and they were in heat. Weren't we all.

I usually get intimidated by people who are so much older than me, because getting old is hard, but these bitches didn't know what they were messing with. I was a horny twenty-one-year-old with a Halle Berry haircut (the short one) who had been funny her whole life and never been sexually desired by a sexy man before, so they could just fuck right off. #feminism.

After the verbal warning from Denise, she and her friends Brenda, Carol, and Margo all went to town on him. There was gyrating, hair flicking in his general direction, and a lot of over-the-top laughing at his terrible slurred jokes. (I fucking love my husband, but calm down, ladies; he's hot, he's not Will Ferrell.) Like any warm-blooded human with fifty gallons of alcohol and God-knows-what-else in his system, he was playing up to their advances. Yep, my future husband was a stripper pole, and I was more than happy to watch the show. But the romance wasn't lost: while he was playing up to the blue-rinse section's advances, he made sure to involve me.

He came over to me, and while I gave him his fifteenth shot of vodka (on the house), he grabbed the tip jar. With a cheeky grin, he walked back over to the seniors set and announced in a loud voice to his audience: "If you ladies give me five dollars, I'll lift my shirt up." With that, fifty dollars' worth of five-dollar notes went flying into the tip jar. MY TIP JAR. He was getting ME tips. I didn't care if he was getting me gonorrhea, he winked at me as he lifted his shirt and I was caught hook, line, and sinker.

I'm not great around guys I'm interested in. I get weird, I insult them and play hard to get, not successfully. Unfortunately I completely buy into the stereotype that you gotta treat them mean to keep them keen. I keep hoping insults and general derogatory remarks about their pimply faces are what will win them over. However, turns out when you're average-looking and a bit frigid, this doesn't cut it. This attitude doesn't get you the desired result, especially on the Gold Coast when surrounded by surfers and footballers.

But with this guy, this future #hothusband, it was different. After my shift I kicked out the hopeful future ex-wives club, and Api and Craig stuck around to help clean up. I changed out of my uniform and into a casual cutoff denim skirt, tan suede boots with a wedge that came just over the knee, and a satin khaki singlet top with cream fringing around the bust. Hello, early 2000s; it was a look that made #hothusband say in later years that when he saw me dressed like that he knew I must have been a confident lass. Api and I hadn't had a real conversation, but earlier in the night he was showing his lady friends his nipples to get me tips and was smiling at me a whole heap, so in horny twenty-one-year-old-speak this meant we were married.

We headed off to the local shit pub that was open later than the shit pub I was working in. I ordered two Malibu and pineapple juices, skulled them both in an attempt to catch up, and channeled my inner Beyoncé ("skulled" is "chugged"—please take note of this as I seem to talk about skulling/chugging a lot of things).

I went up to him, lifted his head, which was resting on the wall while he was dancing, and said, "You'll be coming home with me tonight."

Yes, I fucking did, I said those words, you guys. Just straight to his beautiful face. There was no awkward talk about tampons. No jokes about how hot people don't need to try to be good in bed—they don't have to try to be good at anything else, so why start in the bedroom? Just straight to the point, super sexy and super cool.

He loved it, kissed me hard on my mouth, and we sashayed away together.

As they say, the rest is history, only it isn't.

The next day, as he was leaving my house, DAYUM!

We exchanged numbers—well, I gave him my number, but he decided to give me the *wrong* number because he was still drunk from the night before and couldn't remember his name, let alone ten specific numbers (well, that's what he tells me anyway). Lucky he's pretty, and lucky he called me two days later and we arranged to meet up again.

He was living with his two daughters week on, week off, six hours north of me. So the weeks he wasn't with the girls he would come down to Sydney for a week of work and Celeste. It was great.

We kept the long distance going for eighteen months, and when his situation changed with the girls, he ended up coming to Sydney and moving in with me.

It was the first time I had ever lived with a boyfriend, and I was super excited at the idea of him coming home to my house whenever he wanted and that he would even have his own key.

I had it all sorted out: I was going to be a fun aunty and evil stepmum for the rest of time. I was never going to have kids, no sirree Bob! It's not like I didn't want them; I just didn't think I'd be very good at the whole mothering thing and therefore thought not having them was the answer. I wanted to focus on my career and never damage my perfect size 14 physique. But sometimes the universe and heaps of unprotected sex with Api have different plans for you.

I was living in Bondi with my best friend Jo when I found out I was pregnant with my first son, Lou. Api and I weren't technically together at the time; we were on a break and it was hard. I loved him so much, but our lives were so different. We had been together for seven years, and after living together for four of them, the situation with his daughters changed and he needed to be with them full-time, so he moved away to be with them. I really wanted to get my career cracking, so after three years of long distance, we broke up and it broke our hearts.

I had just got back from a month in America trying to get some shit happening with my career. I cried every day I was over there, missing Api and sad I wasn't coming home to him.

The day before I went to America, Api and his little brother, Zac, were given bravery awards by the Governor General for saving their friend's life after he fell from a cliff. It was such a special day. Even though Api and I weren't together, his mum wanted me there, as I was still "family," and didn't I weasel my way back into that family. The day the bravery award was issued to the Robin boys, Api got me nice and pregnant.

The day I found out, I hadn't had my period for six weeks but just put it down to my body adjusting to life in Bondi, where one must appear undernourished enough that one forgets to bleed.

Turns out that wasn't the case.

Before the urine hit the stick there were two bright-red lines screaming: "YOU'RE PREGNANT, WOMAN!"

What?!?! WHAT!? Pregnant? But I couldn't be. I mean, sure, every time Api and I would see each other we would cry about how much we missed each other over three bottles of wine, naked. But I'm not meant to be pregnant! Am I?? AM I?!? I walked out of the bathroom in Jo's and my tiny, crappy apartment with carpet that smelled like cat urine, kicked open Jo's bedroom door, and screamed at her: "I'M FUCKING PREGNANT."

Without missing a beat she got up and started jumping up and down, singing, "We're having a baby! We're having a baby!"

I was happy she was stoked, because I was numb.

I couldn't believe it. I didn't know what to do. So, in classic Jo Cash fashion she got busy and looked after me. She told me to lie down while she made me banana and honey on toast, rubbed my feet, and booked me a doctor's appointment. And like the perfect friend she was, she said she would go with me to the appointment. But as I had just finished watching back-to-back *Sex and the City* episodes on the flight back from America, I thought as a sign of independence, I should do everything on my own. Dumb pregnant feminist.

Api had gone back home, and I knew I had to tell him but I was scared. I was more scared about telling *him* than I was about telling my parents. (In my mind I'm seventeen and still living at home with my mum and dad, asking if it's OK to finish off the last bit of milk.)

I called him, and it was horrible. It's one of my big regrets in life.

I'm not someone who lives without regrets. I know it's something that some people wear as a badge of honor, "living a life without regrets," but I'm not one of those people. I have a list of them.

I regret not going and visiting my sister when my niece was first born and was in the hospital for the first twenty days of her life with a rare lung disease.

I regret not working harder when I was younger at being an extra on *Friends*.

I regret leaving Sydney during the 2000 Summer Olympics because "Sydney can't handle peak-hour traffic so I don't know how it expects to handle hundreds of thousands of people descending on it for two weeks." Turns out it was "the best Olympics ever," a fact that my dad never lets me forget.

I regret some of the ways I treated my stepdaughters when they were younger and needed me to be better for them.

I regret not backing myself when I was younger and some boys didn't laugh at my jokes because I wasn't fuckable.

I regret not asking Thomas to be in my bridal party.

I regret the way I told Api I was pregnant with our first boy. I don't regret having regrets. I don't see them as things I should be ashamed of; they are things that make me work on decisions I make in the future. Next time my sister calls me and says she needs me, I'll be there. I'm consciously trying to be a better stepmum, friend, and role model to my stepgirls. When Api and I renew our vows, Thomas will be front and center, and I'm currently working toward a guest role on the rebooted *Will and Grace*.

And when I told Api I was pregnant with our second boy, it was such a lovely time. My beautiful friend Nic and I went to the local shopping center to get a pregnancy test. I wanted to go straight to the public toilet to do the test when Nic proclaimed, "No, no, we're not sixteen." So she drove me home; I peed on the stick, ran out of the toilet, told Nic; we jumped and hugged, then told Api, who poured himself and

Nic a very large glass of something while I proceeded to eat the contents of the house.

See? Progress!

But the first time round, I called Api and screamed down the phone that I was pregnant and that I was obviously not going to keep it!

All I wanted to do was have this baby with the man I loved, but I was scared. Scared, emotional, and mean.

I don't even remember what he said. I was hysterical. I slammed the phone down and made my way to the doctor's appointment on my own, in a pair of Manolos.

When I got to the doctor, she pulled out a fancy *Wheel of Pregnancy* fortune wheel, spun it a few times, moved it back and forth, and as I waited for a new car with reclining seats to be handed to me by a woman named Jennifer in a red bikini, my palms started to sweat. There was no car, no Jennifer, and no red bikini. Instead, I was six weeks pregnant. I had no idea what this meant. She may as well have said I was crowning by the way I responded. I didn't know what to do.

My doctor told me that I had options, and I knew exactly what that meant, and I was equal parts relieved and terrified by it. I left the doctor with two pieces of paper. One was a referral to an obstetrician and the other was a referral to an abortion clinic. An abortion clinic! Fuck, I didn't want that, but I didn't know if I wanted a baby. I loved Api so much and I knew what I *didn't* want to do, but I had no idea what Api would want so I was freaking out.

NB I am pro choice, pro women, and pro people shutting the fuck up and leaving us to make our own informed decisions on what's right for our own amazing bodies.

I'm pretty sure he was texting and calling me for the rest of the day, but I didn't answer or respond. It's all a blur. I was in the world of blurriness and didn't have any idea how to find clarity.

Then clarity came in the form of my Maori Adonis.

The next morning, he turned up on my doorstep unannounced. This is not like Api at all, but he knew I needed him and he was there. Even after the way I told him about being pregnant, he still drove six hours to be with me because he knew that was what I needed. *I* didn't even know what I needed.

I was still in bed, and Jo let him in. He opened my bedroom door with a bunch of wildflowers that he had randomly picked on the way over (classic Api) and a vegetable juice.

He kissed and kissed and kissed me until I couldn't be kissed any longer and said how excited he was for us to have a baby together. Well, at least that's what I think he said; it was the middle of summer, and he had his shirt off so I wasn't really paying attention to his words. I could hear Jo sobbing outside my bedroom door, and I knew everything would be all right—better than all right. I knew everything would be fucking awesome.

He proposed to me when I was four months pregnant with our first boy. He cried, I cried, I called Jo straightaway, and she cried. Api and I had been together for ten years when he proposed, overlooking a beautiful beach on the Mid North Coast of New South Wales after watching *Black Swan* (confused face emoji).

Fourteen years together and he's just getting hotter. It's really annoying. Sometimes I set my alarm for the middle of the night just to wake up and look at him, not because I'm a hopeless romantic but more because I want to catch him off guard. I hope to roll over at 3:00 a.m. and see that he's actually one of those people who sleeps with their eyes half-open, sporting a double chin, and has a nose covered in whiteheads along with an uneven jawline.

But no, he's divine. He sleeps with his eyes closed, there are no secret nighttime pimples (he gets pimple breakouts BEHIND HIS EARS!), and he even has a small smile on his sleeping face. We don't need to leave a light on in the house at night for the kids because my husband is a constant ray of fucking sunshine and he glows in his god-damned sleep.

The best part about being with someone so much hotter than me, aside from the crippling fear that he will leave me for a Hadid sister and the horrible insecurities that I wake up with every morning, is that people love to tell me just how hot he is and how lucky I am.

We were at a kids' party, and I was sitting next to a well-dressed older lady who was looking longingly at my eldest son and husband in much the same way as I was looking at the lolly table.

"Your son is a handsome boy."

"Thank you."

"He really is a looker, isn't he?"

"Well, I think so, but I'm a bit biased."

(Polite laughter.)

"He's the spitting image of his father. You didn't get a look-in, love."

"Well, I think there is a little bit of me in him."

"No, I don't think so at all. You must be happy he chose you to have children with. I'm going to have to tell the girls about him at bridge on Wednesday. Would you like some more cake, love?"

Being married to someone universally hotter than I am has opened up a new form of communication with people who wouldn't usually give me the time of day. I once had a lovely middle-aged woman named Brenda cross a busy street to congratulate me on how well I've done by "holding on to my husband." The hardest part about it all is I'm not an insecure person, and certainly not a jealous one, but since Brenda's congratulatory remark I question even the smallest activity he wants to undertake on his own, because I've started drinking the Kool-Aid and think I'm lucky that someone so attractive wants to be with me.

#hothusband: I'm going to get some milk.

Me: Why?

#HH: What?

Me: Why are you getting milk?

#HH: Because you asked me five minutes ago to go and get some milk.

Me: Oh, OK. Thanks.

(He starts to walk out the door.)

Me: Put a shirt on!

#HH: I have a shirt on.

Me: Well, put another one on. And take the kids.

#HH: I'm only going to get milk.

Me: I don't care, take all the kids, and I'm pretty sure the snotty toothless kid from next door is playing out front, so take him as well.

#HH: Are you serious?

Me: Sure am! Oh, and Rollerblade there. No one wants to fuck someone who rollerblades!

#HH: Have you been drinking?

Me: No.

#HH: I'll get you some wine.

Me: Thanks.

Have you ever had an argument with a pretty person? Not like when you have a full face of makeup on and argue with yourself in the mirror about whether Kim Kardashian is a bad influence on young girls or the new enhanced face of feminism.

No, not *those* arguments. I mean *real* arguments. The ones where the two of you go back and forth passionately debating your points of view, then when you're about to make a point that will change the minds of people far and wide you get completely overwhelmed with how pretty your opponent is so you start a whole new argument based solely on the injustices of their perfect cheekbones. Yep, *those* arguments.

Well, I *married* those goddamned cheekbones.

I realized early on in our relationship that ground rules needed to be laid. It was only fair that we started off on the same page. We both have our strengths, and we need to play to them. Stick to our lanes.

I am funny. He is hot. These are very important conversations that need to be had in any relationship, and I think they need to be had early on. Around the same time as the "Are you serious about flannelette sheets all year-round?" and "Do you wee in the shower?" conversations. Nothing is worse than when one party feels they can do a crossover.

Much like a model turned actor, it seems like a great idea but turns out to be kind of embarrassing and leaves people feeling betrayed.

I like that he makes others feel confident enough to tell me how lucky I am. I guess I should wear my tap shoes around more and really turn the tables on who's the "lucky" one.

NB My husband is excellent. If I'd met him on *Kiss Bang Love*, I would have kissed him blindfolded and married him on the spot. He's kind, smart, caring, and very, VERY patient. He's a fun dad and has really thrown his back into tolerating me. I love him with all the wine in the fridge.

Dear Wine

Thank you.

Thank you for your understanding when I need you in my hand during all the witching hours.

Thank you for not being bitchy when I decide to have a "night off" from you.

Thank you for always, ALWAYS tasting exactly how I need you to after the ill-judged "night off."

Thank you for helping me get through cooking risotto.

Thank you for making my son's home reader so much easier.

Thank you for not being a desirable drink when I was in my twenties and making me wait until I was in my thirties to really appreciate you.

Thank you for being worth the wait.

Thank you for helping me deal with people who are mean to me online. Thank you.

If I had one criticism—well, it's more of a request, and it's not directed at you, because let's face it, you're perfect—it's about your partner Hangover.

Remember when I was younger and you and I would hang out all the time without a care in the world?

There was a group of us—you, me, vodka, sometimes Frangelico would come to the party. Oh God, it was fun. Remember? I'd dance on tables, and you and vodka would make me feel like I was the most amazing person in the world, as true friends do.

I'll never forget the warmth that Frangelico gave me on those cold nights. Have you spoken to Fran lately? I haven't seen him in years. God, they were good times, just the Awesome Foursome.

I miss those days. It's tricky now, because Hangover heard we were partying without him, and he's being an arsehole.

Thanks, bae. I love you, I really do. See you at 5:00 p.m.

C x

The One Where My Heart Was Cut Open

Remember when you were twenty-five? What a time, right? Carefree. Skinny. Enjoying those awesome years of spending money you didn't have. Having sex with people you didn't like. Traveling to places with names you couldn't pronounce.

Me? Well, funny you should ask. I decided twenty-five was a great age to really put my back into having emergency open-heart surgery.

And yes, it was as dramatic as it sounds.

Api and I were living in Balmain, and I was working on *All Saints* as a semiregular. I was also teaching dancing three afternoons a week in Rose Bay to privileged rich kids whose parents' boozy lunches usually ran into the early evening, so they booked in a lot of extracurricular activities for their kids, as they didn't want to seem like bad parents. Full disclosure: I totally respect this way of life, because some of those kids were pricks and I understand why drinking a bottle of prosecco while gazing at the harbor is more appealing than dealing with your attention-seeking middle child.

My classes would run from 4:00 p.m. to 5:30 p.m. in a dark hall filled with RSL chairs and trestle tables. I would get there early and put on Janet Jackson's "I Get Lonely," and we would dance flat out for an hour.

It was awesome. I thought it was a really healthy way to be, as I was exercising and hopefully starting to get fitter. I thought at the time I looked much like Beyoncé in her "Halo" music video, but on reflection I feel Peppa Pig jumping in muddy puddles would have been more of an accurate description.

On top of this thrice-weekly afternoon workout I was walking a lot. Api is an arborist, and most of his work was about a thirty-minute drive away, so he would be up and out of the house at 6:30 a.m., and I started getting up and out at this same time. I would like to say it was such a lovely routine to be in and that this time of the morning really is glorious, but I'd be lying. I wanted to stay in that warm bed because I DONT DO MORNINGS! Part of Api's morning routine was to make himself a coffee at home, and the screaming and gurgling of the coffee machine would jolt me out of bed, and if I hadn't gotten out of the house instantly, I would have killed him with frothy milk. Five days a week, I'd do the same routine and walk over the Anzac Bridge and back—a fifty-minute round trip.

I was really happy with my progress and thought I was getting fit. Only I wasn't. I wasn't getting my time down, and I wasn't finding it easier or looking at a new, more challenging walk that included hills and stairs. Instead I was getting a sore left arm, tightness in my chest, and heart flutters. I know, sounds fun, right? Did I mention I was twenty-five?

I called my mum, telling her about my symptoms. She freaked out and said she would fly down from the Far North Coast and come to all the doctor's appointments with me, but being the independent twenty-five-year-old I was I wanted to prove I was a big girl and do it on my own. Silly little girl.

I booked to see my GP. She listened to my heart, and I was told it was "all good," but because of my symptoms she sent me off to see a fancy cardiologist. Still refusing my mum's offers to fly down and attend the appointment with me, I booked myself in to see a cardiologist, Dr. Bruce

Wilson. He was such a beautiful man, who replaced words like "temperature" with "sweat" and "MRI" with "overpriced photos of your insides."

While I ignored texts and calls from my mum to see how I was doing—"Jeez, Mum, I've totally got this" (eye roll emoji)—Dr. Wilson told me I had a hole in my heart.

I wish my mum were here.

"Not only is it a hole—it's a bloody big, gaping hole that is just over 2.5 centimeters in diameter."

Right, OK, sure.

Dr. Wilson could see that I was upset; I think the snot streaming down my face and me screaming "I WANT MY MUM!" at the top of my lungs gave me away. He told me that it could be fixed with a stent, so I demanded to meet Stent immediately to find out what his plan was.

Well, it turned out Stent wasn't a Wizard Doctor, it was a thing to go in my heart.

I have put together a detailed, accurate, and precise description, sourced from many creditable medical journals, of what exactly a stent is, and a clear outline as to how it needs to be inserted. Apologies to those of you who don't understand medical jargon, as this description is full of it.

Stent

A stent is a bit of fabricky stuff that some fancy doctors whack into your heart to cover the dumb hole. They make a tiny cut in your thigh (as this is the obvious choice when thinking of accessing your heart) so they can shove the fabricky thing up through your femoral artery (that's a vein that runs from your groin to your heart—gross). The fabricky stuff is attached with either a peg or a bull clip—depends on what is closest and has been warmed up—to a long bit of wiry, stringy stuff. It is then shoved in the vein. The fabricky stuff somehow gets stuck to the big, dumb, gaping hole in your heart that has prevented you from kissing, ahem, challenging Usain Bolt.

It then dismounts from the peg/bull clip much like pole-vaulters dismount from their poles. Using a natural organic form of superglue, or Elmer's glue for children, it gets stuck over the hole.

The whole process, including the totally invasive and highly uncomfortable shaving of the groin area by an in-your-face nurse named Heather, takes around ninety minutes, two hours if you have quite the bush. You then go back to your ward with other attractive patients who are also rocking the pale-blue hospital gown, eat all the jelly on offer, get food poisoning from the other nondescript hospital food, then head home that night via the pharmacist with a packet of anti-shit-your-pants medication.

You're welcome.

After the news, I called my mum straightaway and screamed down the phone at her, "I'M GOING TO DIE!"

She screamed back at me, "YOU SHOULD HAVE LET ME COME TO THE APPOINTMENT!"

"I KNOW, I'M SORRY, I'M DYING!!!!"

After the screaming, and realizing I wasn't in fact dying, we devised a plan.

I booked in to have the procedure in a few months on a Friday at 11:00 a.m. I'd fast the day before, have it done, go home to rest over the weekend, and be back on set filming my freshly stitched heart out on Monday. BAM! Let's do this!

So, Mum flew down as planned to hang out with Api while I was shaved, cut, dismounted in, and fixed.

We all went in, Dr. Wilson came and greeted us, Heather got busy with her disposable razor, I was knocked out with some sweet, sweet drugs, and Mum and Api went and got a coffee.

Great. I love a plan.

Here's where it gets fun, super fun. After the tiny incision in my groin, the fabric thing made its way to my heart. Tops. However, as it was setting up for the dismount, it kind of went, as they say in all the medical journals, tits up. It went completely fucking tits up.

The little fabric fucker didn't dismount the way it was supposed to, and instead of attaching itself nicely to my heart hole and scoring a high 8.9 out of a possible 9, the little fucker made a half-arsed attempt and only connected to one section of the massive gaping hole in my heart. WHAT. THE. FUCK?

Stupid little fabric thing! That isn't what was supposed to happen. So it needed to be bloody pulled out. Annoying, all the shaving, cutting, FASTING, for nothing.

It needed to be pulled out, and I needed to be woken up to "chat about my options." Fine, another plan. I mean it's a definite plan B, but a plan nonetheless. I'm on board. As the Wizard Doctors were pulling the dodgy little fucker out, instead of it getting its shit together and realizing it hadn't done anywhere nearly as much as it was expected to do so should just accept defeat and cooperate, it decided to not only be a failing little fucker but a stubborn one at that. It snapped off. THE STUPID, FAILING, STUBBORN LITTLE FABRIC FUCKER SNAPPED OFF IN MY HEART AND WAS JUST DANGLING THERE LIKE A LONELY HOEBAG. (I've had a lot of counseling about it. I'm good, you guys.) WHAT. THE. *ACTUAL.* FUCK?

Jump-cut to Api and Mum having an overpriced coffee in an unsterile hospital while they discuss, well, me.

Mum: So, what are your plans?

#hothusband: Well, I really love your daughter, and I can see a beautiful future with her.

Mum: No, not about her, about your hair. How long are you planning on keeping these dreadlocks?

#HH: Um, well, I haven't really given much thought to it.

(Awkward pause.)

#HH: I think Celeste is really funny.

Mum: And pretty.

#HH: And kind.

Mum: Brave.

#HH: And smart.

(Look, I wasn't there, but I'm pretty sure the way I've written this conversation is spot-on.)

Then Mum's Nokia rang.

If this were an episode of *24* and we were filming it in real time, this scene would take place 1.5 hours after the Failing Stubborn Little Fucker scene (and I'd play Kiefer Sutherland's role, goddamn it!).

In her understandable optimism, Mum thought, "Our funny, pretty, kind, brave, and smart girl must be done. Let's head on up and make fun of her while she comes out of the anesthesia." Instead, she and Api were summoned to have a talk with the doctors.

As they walked up the stairs and rounded the corner, they were met by five surgeons—I like to call them the Boy Band of Doctors—standing in scrubs. "Mrs. Barber, there has been a complication with the surgery. We need to talk to you in a quiet room."

Well, talk about going from zero to BATSHIT CRAZY in 0.4 seconds.

The following is a direct transcript of how the conversation that followed played out.

Mum: A quiet room? Why do I need to go to a quiet room?

Doctor 1: Well, the stupid, failing, stubborn piece of shit stent—

Doctor 2: Piece of shit.

Doctor 1: —has malfunctioned.

Api: Fuck.

Doctor 1: It's broken off in her heart. She needs emergency open-heart surgery so we can get it out.

Mum: Malfunctioned? Emergency open-heart surgery?

Doctor 1: Yep, it's snapped off in there. We need to wake her up to get consent to cut her open, but if we do that one of three things could happen.

Mum: OK.

Api: Fuck.

Doctor 1: When we wake her up and take the tube out of her throat, she will cough, and the stupid failing stubborn piece of shit stent—

Doctor 2: Such a piece of shit.

Doctor 1: —will lodge in her heart and (A) she could have a stroke—

Mum: What!

Api: Fuck.

Doctor 1: —(B) she could have a heart attack—

Mum: Please stop talking.

Api: Oh fuck.

Doctor 1: —or (C) it could be fatal.

Mum: STOP TALKING!

Api: FUCK! What should we do?

Doctor 1: Well, you are down as next of kin, so you could sign the consent—

Mum: GIVE ME THE GODDAMNED PEN!!

Api isn't a man of many words. This is one of the things I love about him—well, that and his ability to hold his breath for five minutes. That's amazing; I'm flat out breathing while I eat.

In our relationship, I'm more of the talker and he's the listener. He's hot and I talk; we are very clear about our roles. I believe that talking *at* someone with great urgency at all times, whether it be about the children missing their vaccine appointment or putting the toilet paper roll on UPSIDE DOWN, is a good and healthy form of communication.

Turns out it's not. I know—I'm as shocked as you are, ladies! I spoke to the great Noni Hazlehurst about this when we were shooting *The Letdown*. (To my fabulous non-Australian readers, google Noni

Hazlehurst; once you have seen her incredible body of work, pour a glass of wine and then google Noni reading *Go the Fuck to Sleep*. You will thank me later.)

We were at a pub drinking after a day of filming, and Noni, being excellent and interested, asked me about me and my life. Well, bloody hell, Noni, let me show you some photos. I pulled out my phone—ha, who am I kidding? I was filming the entire conversation, because Noni!

I was showing her photos of my sons, and at the time I had been working away a bit and missing all of them, and Api wasn't sending me texts every ten minutes as I had expected. So I confided in My Noni (that's not a typo, she's mine): "He's amazing, and I love him so much; it's just a bit tricky sometimes because he doesn't talk much."

After which she looked at a photo of him, eyed me over the brim of her sunglasses, and responded, "Well, he doesn't bloody need to when he looks like that, does he, love?"

You're right, Noni, he doesn't, thank you. Ah, reverse sexism is the best!

So when I was told about the hole in my heart we had a conversation about what it might be like. What if for some reason I had to have heart surgery? I was twenty-five and looking down the barrel of an invite to the Logies, so a massive zipper scar running from my throat to my sternum wasn't part of my pre-Logie prep. We like to think the Logies are the Australian Oscars, but it's more like the Razzies. We never discussed this further. It was all hypothetical, because only morbidly obese eighty-year-old men have emergency open-heart surgery, right?

Here is where Api was swiftly upgraded to #hothusband. After Mum had signed the papers and the Boy Band of Doctors was walking away to slice and dice me, Api stepped up, and he stepped up in a big way.

He stopped them and asked, "Is there any other way you can cut her rather than straight down her chest?"

Holy shitballs, Batman! This is the most important question anyone has ever asked on my behalf in my life—well, this and once when my dance teacher asked if I really needed that extra cookie.

The head of the Boy Band of Doctors, Dr. Justin Timberlake, said that aside from the standard Zipper Cut they could perform the "Clam Cut." Mmmm, sexy. The Clam Cut is a massive fuck-off cut that's made underneath your breasts in the same shape as the underwire of your bra. (For those of you who don't wear bras, imagine a cut that goes straight across your chest where your itsy-bitsy string bikini goes, or where your nipple tassels skim your rib cage.)

This was such a massive request. Api knew it was important to me, but he also was worried, because the Clam Cut is a lot more involved and the recovery is more intense. But that's what they went with.

It's been ten years since the operation, and I'm all about the deep V neckline thanks to Api.

The Gross Part

If this was in an issue of *Playboy* magazine, the following would be in the sealed section—so if you get queasy and/or are scared of words like "saw," "drilling," and "severed," then you, my friend, need to skip this bit and come back and find me when I tell y'all about getting totally fucked up on morphine.

As the original surgery was supposed to be routine and only take 1.5 hours, I was given a light Lindsay Lohan circa 2007 type of general anesthetic, just enough of a buzz to knock me out so I wouldn't feel any of the bad stuff and would remember only select details the day after.

But because the Failing Stubborn Piece of Shit stent (such a piece of shit) decided to rear its ugly head, it was time to play with the big boys of operations, and I needed to be sedated a heap, like, a whole lot more. I was now in the territory of Charlie Sheen and his playboy model wives type of sedation.

I was sedated to the extent that my body temperature was lowered significantly and my heart was slowed right down. Slowed down, then stopped, but I was still alive—now, if that isn't proof enough that I had the idea of *The OA* before Brit Marling, I don't know what else you want from me. While slowing me down, they also cooled me down; they needed to slow the beating of my heart so they could put a clamp on it to stop it from beating and then slice it up real nice.

I was essentially turned off and pumping on a machine next to me; how very Bionic Woman of me.

Now it gets really full-on. After the hit of good stuff, they cut me open. A lovely, clean, clam-like cut was made right across my chest. Looking at my scar, I think it was one long slice, which in itself was no mean feat. They then peeled my skin up and over my rib cage, breasts, and right up over my sternum.

So from here, I believe the doctors requested "The Final Countdown" to be blared across the operating room as they pulled out the *Saw*, another movie I thought of first. Dr. JT proceeded to saw my sternum in half, from top to the bottom. This is nothing new in the open-heart surgery game; this is why the zipper has the scar it does, because Dr. JT usually saws straight through the skin and sternum all at once. I'm certain that this is done to cut down on time so he can get back to the doctors' lounge and count his number one hits.

After the saw had been put away, thank God, it was on to the ribs. I've never really thought much about my ribs. The only other time in my life I worried about the well-being of my ribs was when I was dancing and we had to do back bends and I couldn't do them for as long as some of the other spectacular bendy girls. Oh, and I often wondered in my younger years if that rumor that Marilyn Manson had his rib cage removed so he could perform fellatio on himself was in fact a rumor. But aside from that I never really gave the old ribs a second thought. Kind of like my ears—I knew they were there to serve a purpose, but they weren't a focus, like my legs or eyelashes. But now my ribs are on my mind constantly. When I hug my kids I can feel them; when I lie down, I can feel them. My kids even know to say to one another, "Don't hug Mum too hard; it will hurt her chest" (sad face emoji).

My lovely ribs were cracked—I like to say "popped open," because the word "pop" makes me think of the popcorn song, and that song makes me happy, so I won't think of the horribly invasive surgery that changed my life forever.

They had to crack open my rib cage to access my heart. (I'm pretty sure that's the title of Taylor Swift's new album: *Crack Open My Rib Cage to Access My Heart*, ft. Billy Ray Cyrus.)

Once they could access my heart, this was when the cooling-down and heart-stopping stuff happened. You see, they needed to get the Failing Stubborn Piece of Shit out.

Once I was chilled and put on ice, they placed a clamp on the valve to stop the flow of blood to my heart and stop it from beating/moving. They cut open my big, juicy, all-loving heart, retrieved the Failing Stubborn Piece of Shit, and threw that bitch in the bin.

They then cut out a piece of my heart that wasn't being used and used it to sew up the hole. And, voilà, I'm a real girl.

Then comes the "let's put this talented puzzle back together" game. First, I was warmed up, then sped up; then all the crap that had been pulled out and moved around had to be shoved back in. Five holes were drilled through my sternum, and wire was fed through to keep it all in place; then they pulled my skin back over my chest and stitched me up nice and proper.

Then I was off to see the Wizard, the wonderful Wizard of Morphine.

◆　◆　◆

Welcome back, queasy friends, I trust you had a nice break and are feeling fully refreshed and hydrated. Spare a thought for your not so "soft" mates who stuck around through the tough bit and will remain by my side forever and always.

So it turns out the intensive care unit is the most horrible place in the history of the world, which was a shock to me, considering I once worked as the only female writer and cast member on a football show, so I'm familiar with horrible places. Coming out of the Charlie Sheen haze was not only horrible but also frightening.

I felt as though I were underground, in a massive dark tunnel. I was so deep underground that I could feel the density of the earth around me. It was cold, dark, and wet, and I had an overwhelming sense of being alone and terrified.

I was cold, so cold. I started to hallucinate, and not in the good way. I could hear Mum and Api in the distance, but I couldn't reach or connect with them. There was so much going on where they were, and I was alone listening to the chaos from what felt like a million miles away.

I was in so much pain that I couldn't move, and I was desperate to get to them. I was screaming out to them, and they wouldn't listen to me.

Turns out the screaming I was doing was actually silent shrieks that Mum and Api had to sit and watch for a couple of hours until my body had heated up enough for the tube down my throat to be removed. I was cold and alone screaming for my mum and had a terrifying feeling that I was being chased and couldn't escape.

Although the pain was overwhelming, I think the shock of the whole ordeal had made me numb. I was in shock—shock because I was supposed to be having routine surgery and instead was woken up seven hours later in recovery from emergency open-heart surgery.

I have never felt so alone in my life. It was truly horrible. I have told this story so many times, and I've got it down to a fine art, but sitting here writing it (over poached eggs and a latte #blessed), it still shakes me up, and I'm still sad for little brokenhearted Celeste.

Finally, as I was coming out of the anesthesia, I remember I could hear my mum and Api faintly in the background, while the nurse was screaming in my ear: "CELESTE! CELESTE, CAN YOU HEAR ME?!"

Jesus, did she think I'd had a cochlear implant fitted and felt the need to test it out?

Dr. Timberlake was right: the recovery from this surgery was a big old turd. Those of you who have had emergency open-heart surgery at twenty-five due to a Failing Stubborn Piece of Shit will know that the nursing staff thinks it is a genius idea to get you up and walking the day after the slice-and-dice. Of course they do. But why stop there? Why not get me training for the pole-vault tournament that the Failing Stubborn Little Fucker couldn't achieve?

Oh, but the silver lining, the sweet, sweet silver lining of this monumental medical fuckup was the plethora of hospital-grade drugs that were pumped directly into my broken body. I'm sure the total street worth of the shit I had pumping through my veins would have made Pablo Escobar reassess his alliances.

I was originally on morphine, but it wasn't agreeing with me. I mean it was knocking me the fuck out and I couldn't really feel anything, but I was operating in two states of consciousness. I either felt dizzy and nauseous, or I would hallucinate that terrorists were plotting to kidnap me. We decided to take me off morphine, and by "we" I mean "everyone else in the world other than me" because I was flat out trying to stay upright on a chair and not pass out, let alone make any big decisions. I had chest tubes that were sewn into my chest to drain the twelve kilograms of fluid I had gained in twenty-four hours post-surgery. I had a central line inserted in my neck that fed directly into a large vein. This is where the nurses would administer my drugs and fluids. I also had a catheter, which is a tube that is shoved through your bits into your bladder.

The doctor spoke with the pain management team about taking me off morphine and putting me on a high dose of Endone. They discussed my chest tubes and what they should do regarding extra pain relief when they were removed. I distinctly remember overhearing the doctor talking to my mum, saying, "Let's give her some wall greens and a flower before her boobs pop out, because that ship is faithful."

Turns out he actually said, "Let's give her some morphine an hour before the tubes come out, because that shit be painful."

Whatever, I was high.

Three days after this exchange, I was acclimatizing to my new drug program (i.e., not shitting at all when it came time to have the tubes removed). Nurse Ratched came in announcing that "today is the day," which I was excited and nervous about. Happy to be rid of the tubes but also a bit worried about the pain. Both my mum and dad were at the hospital, and in classic Dad style he stood outside, out of the way, but still giving his love and support. And Mum stayed there, solid as a rock, with my sister on the phone checking in every five minutes.

As Nurse Ratched was gloving up for the tube pulling, I stopped her, saying, "Um, the pain management team have ordered some morphine for me to have before the tubes come out."

She said to me, "You don't need it, love; it's not that painful."

If I had been my normal witty self and wasn't out of my face on Keith Richards's stash, I would have said to her, "OK, so you were fine not to have any morphine when you had your chest tubes ripped out after emergency open-heart surgery?" But I wasn't myself. I was fragile, in pain, and under the "care" of medical professionals. With that she snipped the stitch that was keeping the right tube in place and slowly pulled that tube out of me. I have *never* experienced anything like it. It hurt so much that I couldn't scream, I couldn't breathe. All I could do was moan in pain and arch my back in the hope that my chest would explode and I would die. When she was done with the right tube, she walked around the foot of the bed while I sobbed into my mum's arms, begging her not to let the nurse do it again. Before Mum could say anything, the left stitch had been snipped and the tube tugging began. I can't believe I didn't die of pain that day.

Remember where you were when Princess Diana died? I was on a bus on my way back from dancing at the local shopping center in Brisbane. The bus was about to pull out, and I was sitting in the back with Julie East and Sally Parker, counting the number of sequins on our homemade costumes, when we heard on the radio that she had died. I was thirteen, and like any dramatic teenager I began to tell stories about how much more affected I was by her death than anyone else in the world. For the next twelve months I prayed for my future husband, Will and/or Harry; I wasn't picky. What about Michael Jackson? I was on the set of *All Saints*, and the whole crew was watching it on the news as I was walking past and was being told about it by my sister over the phone. I, like any other dramatic twenty-five-year-old, began to tell stories about how much more affected I was by his death than anyone else in the world.

Yep, we all have stories.

As full-on as having emergency open-heart surgery was for me, it seemed just as, if not more, traumatizing for my family and friends. They all have a story.

My sister, Olivia:

> *It was pouring with rain . . . like completely pissing down, and I was in New Farm (Brisbane) driving with my son, Harry, who was maybe ten weeks old. Mum called me and I had to pull over. I was in complete shock but didn't feel anything—I didn't know what to feel. I called my husband, Ben, and he was beside himself and left work early.*

Marika (best friend):

I was in a rehearsal room. You and I had spoken that morning, early, before you went in. The phone rang around midday, and I saw your name on caller ID, so I thought you were in recovery and calling for a chat. So I answered the phone and said, "So you're alive, then?" It was Buela calling me on your phone, telling me you almost weren't alive.[9] I was horrified. Panicked. Stayed in the rehearsal but told the director my phone would be on and I would be checking it throughout—something I've never done before or since.

Thomas (best gay):

Fuck, shit, really? Fuck!

I am now known in friendship circles, and some Weight Watchers meetings, as "the Comedian of People's Hearts" or "the Puller of Heartstrings."

So, if you would like to join this group of name-callers, have a little think back to what you might have been doing on August 21, 2007, around lunchtime.

---

9   Buela is what my friends call my mum. For those who don't know it, The Comedy Company was a sketch comedy show in Australia in the '90s, and there were two characters on there called Neville and Buela, and they would always talk about their geriatric sex lives and how they always loved to do everything naked. Since my dad's name is Neville, from the moment that sketch appeared my mates called my mum Buela. She loves it.

The One about My Breasts

During my pregnancy with Lou, the doctors and midwives suggested I call Dr. Timberlake and ask for any additional information on my heart, in case I had missed anything during my morphine phase. I thought while I had the busy surgeon on the phone I would ask about the breastfeeding situation, if there was a situation to be asking about.

I was told that during the surgery, when my skin was peeled up over my chest plate (spew face emoji), my milk ducts were cut—not all of them but most of them—so I *might* be able to breastfeed, but the only way to find out was to "suck it and see." I remembered hearing a few mums and midwives saying that the birth isn't anywhere as full-on and challenging as the weeks and months that follow. Of course I didn't believe it, because if Kourtney Kardashian didn't experience hardships as a new mum, then none of us should. She's the spokesperson for everyday women, right?

But the three months following Lou's birth were some of the most difficult of my life. I wanted to breastfeed so bad. But I just couldn't.

Here's the thing: my body showed no signs of not wanting to feed. All my milk came in, so I looked like a nice dairy cow. I *looked* like I was good to go. All the milk was filling up my bad boys nicely; only it didn't then move on to my son. So when he took to my nipples with a chain saw and vinegar, it was a whole new level of pain that I wouldn't wish on my least favorite Real Housewife.

On the Mid North Coast, where we were living at the time, not only did the midwives believe the idea that Breast Is Best, but they thought that breast was the only option. There were posters all through the hospitals—women breastfeeding six-year-olds in parks, women breastfeeding newborns on roller coasters—and I was told by a number of women that an ideal day with a newborn is lying in bed while they just "suckle at your bosom, and your partner feeds you."

Not. On. Your. Life. I'm pro breastfeeding, but I'm also pro not trying to kill yourself and ruin your newborn's life because you can't cope with the pressures that other women put on you regarding your boobs. Taylor Swift says we all need to support each other, so back the fuck up.

I spent ten full days breastfeeding my son blood mixed with a little breast milk. He cried and cried and cried, he was so hungry (God, that's hard to type without getting upset).

After the ninth day, I didn't know what to do. I was beside myself. I was trying to feed Lou, but it was still the same stabbing pain, and he was still crying and crying and crying.

My sister was visiting, and she saw how terrified and in pain I was. She quietly whispered in my ear, "It's not always going to be like this, I promise."

I burst into tears. This was exactly what I needed to hear. I couldn't believe how horrible the whole experience was, and I was panicking, thinking that this was how my life would be now: I'd always be exhausted, scared, and in pain. I know I'm not the only mother to feel this. Trust me.

As tears ran down my face, Api, who was sitting next to me the whole time, decided he was over it. He stood up and said he was going to the pharmacist to get formula. He couldn't watch me go through this pain when the breastfeeding was clearly not working for me or Lou.

"We aren't doing this, babe. You're beside yourself, Lou is starving, this is bullshit." And with that he left for the chemist. He saved me that day.

My mum was there too. She reminded me that *I* was Lou's mum, and whatever I decided to do was the right thing. So I decided to put Lou on formula, or at least "top him up" until my nipples sorted themselves out.

Api came back from the pharmacy with every conceivable brand of formula for newborns, along with bottles, nipples for the tops of bottles, a sterilizing machine to clean the bottles, and a cleaning machine that cleans the sterilizing machine. We were set.

On this same day, I was expecting a home visit from the midwife, Karen. She was due to come around lunchtime. Lou was meant to have a feed at the same time, and I thought it would be a good opportunity to try him on a bottle of formula, thinking I would have extra support from her.

When Karen arrived, I asked my sister to please put the kettle on so I could get a bottle ready.

Karen wasn't having this. "What's the kettle going on for?"

I froze, like I had been caught stealing chewing gum from the gas station. "Um, I'm having a really rough time with feeding, so I was going to try and see if he will take a bottle."

I was shaking. I could tell she wasn't going to like it, and I wasn't strong enough to back myself.

"No, no, turn the kettle off. We are going to get this baby on your boob."

Fuck, OK, sure. I didn't want to, but she was the expert and this was obviously what was best for my baby. Why else would she be telling me to do it when she saw how exhausted and helpless I was?

I told my sister to turn the kettle off, and I braced myself. I lifted my shirt up and prepared the war zone as best as I could. As she grabbed my restless, hungry baby, I felt my shoulders tense and my toes curl under. She leaned forward and shoved him onto my boob so hard that we, my baby and I, gasped in pain and shock. Then he went to it, chewing on my nipple like it was tobacco and he was at a ball game. I was crying, my mum was crying, my baby was crying, and Api and my sister were pacing. They were pissed off.

The midwife held Lou on my nipple for what felt like forty-five minutes. He was wriggling and chewing, *I* was wriggling and crying, and she just held him there, not letting either of us move. "Everyone finds it hard, love; you've just got to keep at it."

This was it—this was the guilt that was forcing me to do something I couldn't do, the guilt that was making me feel like if I didn't breastfeed my son, then I might as well put vodka in his bottle and inject meth into his veins.

After she had finished manhandling me and my son, she packed up her things and said that when she came back in a week she really wanted to see me breastfeeding, exclusively.

I wanted to breastfeed so much, I really did, but my body just wasn't letting me. I had to trust that putting my son on formula wouldn't be the worst thing in the world.

As soon as Karen left, I changed midwives, and for six months Lou was fed exclusively on formula. It turned out to be the best decision I had made since becoming a mum.

Ladies, trust yourselves, and if you are too sleep deprived to even pull your pants up after going to the toilet and you're scared of making any big decisions, then trust someone who loves you. Someone who knows you, not someone who is paid to push an agenda, or someone who has nipples of steel and was upset that she had to stop breastfeeding her ninth child at the age of eleven because it was getting weird.

We are all different, and even though my boobs look really nice, thanks to emergency open-heart surgery they are bloody useless. But never fear—I'm sure there's room for our steel nipples and useless boobs in Taylor's Squad.

Dear Hangover

Why?

Why do you have to be such an arsehole?

At 5:00 a.m., why do you need to sit behind my left eyebrow and just kick at me?

Kick, kick, kick.

It's not dehydration; it's not alcohol poisoning. It's a few glasses of wine, and you're being a douche about it.

Sunday morning after a long night of some celebratory champagnes, then on to copious cocktails at the local gay bar followed by a red wine nightcap—yep, you are well within your rights to dress in your favorite and most expensive suit and go to town on my head.

But Wednesday morning after a night of sitting on the couch, watching reruns of *RuPaul's Drag Race: All Stars* with two glasses of white wine, is not a party you are invited to.

Also, while I have you, I have one request: when the kids aren't around, can you please, PLEASE fuck off.

I know what you're trying to do. It's so obvious—you're trying to put a wedge between me and Wine, trying to make me regret spending time with him. But you can't. You won't.

What Wine and I have is special, and you just need to deal with it.

Thanks for your consideration, but get fucked.

Celeste

The One about My Mum

Mum had a pretty tough time growing up. Her parents split when she was young, and she fast became one of those kids who would sit on the front step of the pub for hours waiting for her dad every other Saturday when he had her.

My mum is the youngest of three. Her big brother, Bill, is twelve years older than her, and her sister, Christine, is in the middle and six years older. Mum is the baby and the most resilient of all of them.

After her parents split, life became hard for my nana, and she would struggle to keep a job, as my pop would cause a bit of shit around her workplace and she would have to keep changing jobs. "She never got fired," my mum is quick to remind me, a fact that I know she is proud of. "She just had to keep moving around, because being a woman in any kind of industry in the early '60s was hard enough, let alone with your ex-husband trying to cause shit for you."

When mum was ten, Nana got a job as a housekeeper and moved from Sydney to Walcha, a small town just outside Tamworth in the northeast of New South Wales. Billy and Christine had moved out, and Nana couldn't take Mum with her, so Mum was sent to live with her uncle Colin and aunt Irene and her two cousins Collette and Donna in Sylvania in Sydney's south.

Because of the move, Mum had to change schools. She was taken out of Brigidine in Randwick and enrolled into Our Lady of Fatima in Caringbah. Even though Mum attended that school for nearly two years with Donna, she was never bought the new school uniform. For the whole time she was living with her uncle, aunt, and two cousins, she was going to a school where she was wearing a different uniform from everyone else.

Mum lived with Aunt and Uncle for eighteen months, sharing a room with Donna for the entire period.

One morning before school, Mum and Donna were having a fight over breakfast when Donna said, "Well, it doesn't matter anyway. You're going to boarding school, so we don't need to share with you anymore."

With that Mum got up, grabbed Donna by her long red ponytail, and whipped her head around, screaming: "NO, I'M NOT. SHUT UP, DONNA! I'M NOT GOING TO BOARDING SCHOOL!"

Neither had any idea what boarding school was. Mum just knew she wasn't going.

Two months later, Nana picked Mum up and they were off to boarding school. The school was in the same area as Nana's job in Walcha, so Mum was excited to be close to her mum again.

Whenever I ask Mum about how this felt, she is always so kind and understanding toward her mum. "She just did what she had to do."

Mum shared a bed with Nana up until going to live with Aunt and Uncle at age eight; then when she moved to Aunt and Uncle's she slept on the bottom bunk in Collette's room and her clothes were stored in Donna's. This was the living arrangement for two years before she went to boarding school, where she shared a room with eighteen other girls.

My mum loves company; I get this from her. We aren't fans of big crowds or "events," but we like having *our* people around. Whenever I see my mum, we will sit on the couch across from one another, either on our phones or flicking through the glossy mags.

I'll look at her and ask, "Do you want to do anything?"

To which she will usually reply, "Not really. It's just nice having company."

The day before the first day of boarding school, Nana took Mum to the local men's barber, where she insisted all of her hair be cut off. "This is what the school requires, Kathryn—all the girls will be the same," Nana said to Mum, and of course Mum trusted her.

Mum walked out of that barber with hair no more than an inch long all over her head, a style she refers to as "the Mia Farrow."

That afternoon Nana dropped Mum at boarding school a day earlier than anyone else. At the age of twelve she was alone in a new place, staying on her own in the boarding school.

The next morning, the official first day of school in a new town, where she knew no one, with new, shitty short hair, Mum took one look at all the other girls and froze.

All of them had their hair in ponytails. Long ponytails. "Some had navy-blue ribbons in their hair; others needed headbands to hold back the masses of locks from falling onto their faces," Mum will say when she retells this story. "Some had ponytails on the crowns of their heads, and their hair was so long that it went all the way down to their bums."

The new school was Saint Dominica's, or Saint Dom's, as Mum calls it. SIDEBAR: My mum is Queen of Nicknames; everything can either be shortened or lengthened depending on what she's working with, and because my mum LOVES an audience, she will constantly repeat the nickname to cement her street cred. Mum went to school with a girl called Sipple, so she is instantly "Sip," or when Mum is talking about surfing, something she knows nothing about, she will say, "I remember going to the Malfunction Competition with my brother Bill." Most people who talk about such comps have been surfing for at least 5,674,983 years and refer to them as Mal Comps, but not Kath Hemmings, the little girl from Saint Dom's in Tamworth. To her they were the Malfunction Competitions (the MAL-function Competitions).

My uncle Bill had moved to the Gold Coast with his wife, and they had just had a baby. My cousin was born with a number of health issues, so my uncle summoned my nana to go up there and help look after their sick newborn, leaving Mum alone again at boarding school.

During the weekends and school holidays at Saint Dom's, most of the boarders would go home and visit family. Not my mum. Because Nana had moved away to raise her firstborn grandchild, Mum was left alone in Tamworth.

More often than not she was left alone at the boarding school on weekends and holidays. Just her and the nuns.

There was a lovely local girl, Merrilyn Wall (Aunty Mam), who also went to Saint Dom's but wasn't a boarder; she was just a day pup. After a few too many weekends and holidays when Mum was left alone like this, Aunty Mam wasn't having a bar of it anymore and started taking Mum home with her for family get-togethers.

This started a lifelong friendship. Mum and Aunty Mam have been friends so long they even look the same. Aunty Mam and Uncle Ray (who looks like my dad—it's all very weird) are my family's lifeline. Their four kids, Sheeree, Anna, Joel, and DJ, are my brothers and sisters from other misters and mums (I'm pretty sure that's how the saying goes), and I love every red and strawberry blond hair on their perfectly shaped heads.

After boarding school, Mum moved up to the Gold Coast to live with Nana again. On her final day in Tamworth, she got on a bus at 6:00 a.m., on her own, waved goodbye to her boarding family, hugged Aunty Mam until they both cried so hard they snorted, a tradition that they have held on to for the past fifty-one years, and headed north.

When Mum arrived on the Gold Coast she didn't know anyone, just her mum and Father Hoade, the priest from a Catholic church just over the New South Wales border. I met Father Hoade when I went to Saint Joseph's College; he was the kind of man who was born one hundred years old and stayed that age until he died. The only time I would see him was during school Mass, when we would all get buses to the local church. I thank him for the hour-long naps I had in church.

On December 17, 1971 (Kath Barber LOVES a date and time recall), Mum's cousin Collette was up visiting so they went to a party nearby at Tugun with the crew from the local youth club. And didn't they go all out!

Mum wore a long burgundy paisley cheesecloth off-the-shoulder dress (obviously), and Aunty Collette, the cool uni student from Sydney, who is all arms and legs, wore a white skort (Is it a skirt? Is it shorts? No, my friend, it's a skort.), a yellow knit top with blue and orange stripes, and matching striped over-the-knee socks with white clogs, because why wouldn't you?

This is where they met my dad, Neville William Barber. Dad was there with some of his mates when Mum and Aunty Collette walked in. Mum thought that Dad was interested in Collette, but then Kath Hemmings came along and, like all the other good female role models in my life, she shut that shit down.

From the day they met, they saw each other every day. Dad would go around to Mum's place each afternoon after his traineeship as a cabinetmaker. If my nana was still alive, she wouldn't say he was there every day, she'd say he was there EVERY. SINGLE. DAY.

"Doesn't he have a home to go to?" Nana would ask Mum.

"Nup," Mum would say with a smile and a hushed voice, as Dad was no doubt in the next room.

My mum and dad have been together for forty-six years and married for forty-three. When Mum tells me stories of her childhood and growing up, I can't wait to get to the part where she met Dad.

My parents look after each other like no one else can. They get each other, love each other, respect each other, and would happily gang up on me and my sister anytime.

The One about Jo and How I Got in Trouble at Yoga

I met Jo on *All Saints* and, from the moment I met her, I wanted to wrap her and her energy up in a ball, put her in my back pocket, and carry her around with me EVERYWHERE. She was the bee's knees, the duck's nuts, the cat's pajamas, the dolphin's earrings. She was always happy and cheeky and perfect. She was a makeup artist, and *All Saints* was her first big gig.

I really struggle when it comes to writing about Jo, but I couldn't write a book without including her because she was everything to me.

I could tell you about when she was diagnosed with cancer and decided to go to Bali to train as a yoga teacher.

I could tell you how I thought she was crazy and I suggested that, instead of going and doing something as horrible as yoga in Bali and being away from me for any longer than the time it took her to go to the toilet, that she should instead just lie in my bed forever so that I could bring her cups of tea, rub her feet, make her laugh, and do anything possible to take her cancer away.

I could tell you how much I regret not telling her I loved her every single second she was alive.

But I can't. Not yet. It's too hard. And the thought of reliving losing her again is unbearable.

So instead I will tell you about the wonderful, beautiful girl I met on *All Saints*, who EVERYONE loved, and I mean everyone. I will tell you about Jo and the time she finally convinced me to go to yoga with her.

◆ ◆ ◆

While Api and I were broken up, I moved to Bondi Beach with my friend Wil. He and I had lived together before in Coogee with a group of other freshly graduated actors, and we definitely didn't smoke like chimneys and experiment with drugs . . . *you* did!

Living with Wil, or Wilma as I like to steal from *Will and Grace*, was the best. We got a shitty place on the beach at North Bondi because in Bondi you only live in shitty places unless you're a cricketer and can afford a fancy two-bedroom apartment with actual walls. Then Wilma got a fancy job opportunity in Hollywood, baby! and he was on the next plane out of Oz to get his show on the road. After a few months of being in LA he realized he wasn't coming back and would need to officially move out.

I couldn't believe my luck when Jo agreed to move in. Two room-mates at a time in my life when I couldn't have needed them more. Wilma, the best. Then Jo, the best. Me, emotional.

When Jo moved in, it felt like Christmas every day. Every morning she would wake up and come into my room with a cup of tea and wish me "good morning" in her sweetly pitched voice. I would say something about hating mornings; she would laugh and tell me what her plans were for the day, always including me in all of them. On weekends or days off, Jo made me do things I didn't want to do. She made me run and drink green juice and do yoga. No one else in the world has ever or will ever get me to do these three most hated things, and enjoy them.

When we would walk down and get our horrible green juice (aptly named "veggie patch"), Jo would shriek at how I chugged it in two gulps.

Jo: Don't skull it!

Me: It tastes like ass.

Jo: Just sip it.

Me: No way, I want it over and done with.

Jo: You're going to vomit.

Me: Hopefully.

A friend of ours, Mirrah, lived up the road with her boyfriend, Dave. She and Jo would do "soft sand" running together. I think it's because they are sociopaths and were plotting to harm communities, but they said it was to get fit . . . whatever. So they would run up and down the soft sand of Bondi Beach daily. Mirrah is nice and cynical, so I'd enjoy her whinging afterward over a bottle of rosé and a soft-cheese platter. But Jo was always happy and perfect. Nothing was a hassle, and she loved how much I complained about most things—especially yoga.

Mirrah, Jo, and I all worked on *All Saints* together. Mirrah joined the show soon after Mark died, and I thought she was the most beautiful girl in the world—aside from Jo, obviously. After the show was canceled, Jo went onto *Home and Away*, and I was a writer and actor on a football show. We had weird hours, but we would always make time to have a weekly "family" dinner after work at the local Thai restaurant with Mirrah, Dave, and Jo's beautiful boyfriend, Jacky.

Mirrah was just as stoked about the juice and the yoga and all the running as Jo.

Being a university-educated actor (hello, juxtaposition!), I've done a fair bit of yoga. We did it every day at drama school as part of our movement classes. It was intense, and I didn't really believe that holding a pose for what felt like four million minutes would get me to a high spiritual state. There is some good pot that can do that a lot quicker.

Yoga, by definition, is "an ancient art based on a harmonizing system of development for the body, mind, and spirit"—which, when practiced in Bondi or LA, is a way of justifying wearing overpriced clothes and getting out of doing grown-up things.

In the years after drama school, I really liked the *idea* of yoga—chilling out, getting centered, acting as though I'm a superior being because I "practice" daily. All of these things were appealing to me, but I saw it as a chore. It hurt, gave me a headache, and made me realize I'm not as flexible as old boyfriends said I was.

Jo and Mirrah loved yoga. They would go to classes together three times a week while I stayed home and googled simple hot-pot recipes.

I loved these ladies so much, so when they asked me to join them I was equal parts excited and petrified.

Me: Oh, I don't know—yoga kind of freaks me out. I don't think I'll be very good.

Jo: What?! No! You'll be fine.

Mirrah: I'm not very good either; you'll be totally fine. You used to dance, right?

Me: Yep.

Jo: And didn't you do a heap of yoga at uni?

Me: Well, we did, but it was just a series of movements over and over again; it wasn't a crazy class full of bendy models.

Mirrah: Oh, just shut up and come. We can all be shit together.

Me: I don't know . . .

Jo: We can have wine for dinner after class.

Me: SOLD!

As I don't do anything by halves, I jumped in the deep end and got a ten-class pass—yep, that's right, I was going to yoga the shit out of yoga and show it who was boss once and for all. Also, I was living in Bondi, and if you *don't* do yoga when you live in Bondi, people think you are a leper or, even worse, a miner.

So I got my mat, sold my puppy to buy the correct attire, and headed off to my first proper-dopper yoga class.

When Mirrah and I got there the room was so dark and smelled *so good*. Oh God, it smelled good. It smelled like roses and lavender and warm hugs and fried rice. The only form of light was the candles at the front of the room, and some crazy incense gave me that awesome feeling you get when you just finish a sneezing fit. All the people who had just done the previous class were floating around the room putting their personalized mats and blankets away. They spoke to each other with their hands in prayer position, using long, low, one-word sentences and adding the "r" sound A LOT.

Hiiiiii

Namastarrrre

You trrroo

Love yorrruuuuu

Thank yorrruuuu

Coffeeeee??

Yeahhhh

Greaaaaat

This place is fucking bananas.

We found our place on the floor, put our mats down, and I got ready—ready to turn over a new organic yoga leaf.

A very bendy man stood at the front of the class in pants that looked like they were worth more than my uncle's boat. He looked everyone in the eye, welcoming all of us to this sacred space, a space that before today I thought was a dodgy junkyard. Now, I'm not good at eye contact at the best of times, so this individual eye penetration was a confronting way to start something that I was already confronted by.

After the silent eye-sex we were into it. Yoga—not sex. There were people next to me bent in half, attempting to lick their backs, and I did my best to keep up. From back licking we snapped—ahem, *flowed*—into some sort of leg-above-head stuff, and then from there our coccyx attempted to balance on our ear. (NB It was our right ear, of course, because balancing one's coccyx on one's left ear would ruin one's flow and, well, just be silly.)

The people around me, including my yoga traitor friends, had finished the first sequence with ease and were gearing up to go again.

Shit?! How did this happen? What had I missed? I hadn't even had a chance to adjust my activewear out of my camel toe, and we're going again?!

I took a deep breath, and I realized that I was being thrown off by the lack of "five, six, seven, eight" (did I mention I used to dance?), so I thought I'd revert to what I knew. I'd watch the choreo—ahem, *sequence*—watch their moves, take it all in, then catch them up on the next round.

Great, a plan! I'm in business! I'll probably be invited to the front of the class to show my moves and be given a patchouli candle in celebration.[10]

So as my fellow yogis proved that a spine is purely for decoration, I stood silently and watched, tapping my foot along to the beat I'd created in my head.

As I was standing still, I noticed Guru McBendy glide his way over to me. I immediately felt validated; I thought, "Here we go, from one movement expert to another, he can see I've got the posture of a former dancer," and as I began to bend down to roll up my borrowed mat and begin my stride of pride to the front of the class, he stood directly in front of me and through a coconut-milk, decaf-latte breath said, "If you don't know what you're doing, crouch down on your mat and divert your gaze. You're putting people off by just standing there."

With that he eye-fucked me again and glided off.

I couldn't believe it. I had done nothing wrong! Yet I was in trouble. *I got in trouble at yoga.* THIS IS WHY I DIDN'T WANT TO GO. I DON'T BELONG THERE.

As I crouched down on my mat and assumed the fetal position, I looked to Mirrah for support, expecting a "how fucking dare he say that to you" look, or at the very least a "I'm so sorry I dragged you here" vibe. But Mirrah had all of a sudden found her zen, which involved making eye contact with anything and anyone but me.

I stayed in child's pose (a stupid name for a pose, as I've never seen a child in that pose EVER!) until the end of class, sorry, "practice."

There is a twenty-minute meditation at the end of each class when people wrap themselves up in between three and forty-six blankets, put socks and eye pillows on, and lie there like they have actually done a hard day's work in their life. I usually fall asleep in the meditation part of anything, but I was so embarrassed and furious about being yoga

---

10   Fuck patchouli.

shamed that I was tense as hell and stiff as a board, cursing under my breath at every instruction.

Guru McBendy: Now, close your eyes, and take a deep breath in.

Me (in my head): Shut up, dickhead.

G McB: Imagine all the negative energy leaving your body.

Me: I bet you're still wearing the same undies you had when you were twelve.

G McB: Now fill your entire body with warm light.

Me: Your face looks like a dropped pie, fuckhead.

Yep, no one knows rage like a below-average child dancer who is shamed in yoga class.

After class, Mirrah and I recited the goings-on of the class to Jo, laughing hysterically at the bullshit events that we had experienced. Jo was mortified that I had these experiences at her beloved yoga, and Mirrah couldn't really remember any of it because during meditation she managed to fall asleep so deeply that she shocked herself awake by farting.

Jo was brighter than the sun.

She was my best friend, my sister, and one of the greatest loves of my life.

She let me hate yoga, which I'm forever grateful for, and I will love her every single day for the rest of my life.

The One Where I Discover Being Famous on Instagram Is Like Being Rich at Monopoly

I think it's fair to say I'm pretty successful on social media. I'm not getting paid $400,000 to promote detox tea, Kardashian-style (true story), but I've got more than four million Instagram followers, and in my book—and the book of my teenage stepdaughters—that is kind of totally hectic and OMG, like, fully crazy.

I didn't always have a world-famous, highly entertaining Instagram account; I used to have a super-normal account and post really boring photos like most of you. You know the type of photos—ones of my feet, because God knows no one believes you have feet unless they are posted on Instagram; it's the same for breasts and pert bums, so it seems. I'd also post the obligatory food photos, although fortunately no one ever questioned whether I was ever eating to justify posting photos. I'd like to get a bit creative, and I'd post photos of me eating while my feet were also in the pic. Really reinventing the wheel over here, you guys.

Then I had children, so it would have been downright neglectful if I hadn't posted photos of *their* feet. I didn't breastfeed, so there was no point in posting any photos of my children being formula-fed since birth, because I would have been lynched and would be writing this book from a hospital with a bloody syringe as a pen and my upper thigh as the paper. I love Instagram, I really do. I remember when it first came out. "Dropped"? "Hit the market"? "Launched"? "Lost its virginity"? I don't know what the phrase is for the arrival of a new app, but I remember I was excited. As a child of consumerism and the unofficial face of ADD, this shit was right up my alley, because it required the attention span of a cashew nut: approximately five seconds.

You see, I'm a picture-book kind of gal. Words scare me. Sure, they excite me too, but I'm not super smart and I get scared of them. But pictures? Come on! I love them, they are all I need, they can tell a thousand words, right?

I love a good magazine, and Instagram seemed like the digital version of the magazine world: pretty pictures coupled with snappy headlines/captions.

My go-to magazine is *InStyle*. I always loved and collected it—until I had children and realized that *InStyle* and parenting/stepparenting are as compatible as tits on a bull. I had to give one up; turns out trying to give up kids is a little more frowned upon than canceling a magazine subscription. But back in my heyday, when I was living alone in my studio apartment in Kings Cross, I never missed an issue. I had so many that I fantasized about using them as the legs of a coffee table with an old mirror resting on top, creating a super-fancy piece of art/furniture fit for a Tom Ford film. But instead I stashed them under my bed in the hope that the creativity and style would seep through my mattress into my mind during the night.

After a while, as my collection of magazines was getting a little out of hand, instead of just throwing them out like Rihanna might throw out shade, I decided each month I would sit with a family-size packet of Allen's Party Mix lollies and cut out the different sections of the magazine. I would paste them into an overpriced artist's sketchbook I had purchased with the tips I made from being a waitress at a theater restaurant and make my own little *InStyle* highlights each month.

The cover image would go in first; I'd cut out the cover model and paste in the headlines around her, coupled with the date, which I hand-drew in multicolored pencils. (Did I mention I was in my twenties?) Images of what fashions were in season that month followed, and then I would cut out the feature article, and around it I would paste in the images of whatever celebrity was being interviewed and highlight any quotes I found interesting.

The makeup suggestions came next, then the feature on an Australian performer. (This is my favorite part of the Australian *InStyle* magazine; they always do a three-page feature on an Australian entertainer toward the back of the magazine. I still stand in supermarket aisles flicking to the back to see which Australian actor, comedian, model, or writer is being featured this month—"No, still not me? Oh well, maybe next month.") Then I'd finish with the images of houses and food.

My edited version of the magazine would occupy between five and nine pages of my art book, and that was all I needed. Just the pictures; then I knew what was going on.

So when Instagram first dropped? (AHH, here we go again. "Was birthed to the world"? "Popped its cherry"? "Initially assaulted our senses"?), I thought, "Yes! This is the Celeste scrapbook version of Facebook. There will be photos, and that's all I need." How fun—I loved seeing famous people post weird photos of themselves, giving us ordinary peasants a glimpse into their crazy world.

But after a few months of this I became aware that these celebrity lifestyles were starting to be seen as "normal," and a whole new culture of the most ridiculous photos was born.

Images programmed to make us feel like we weren't good enough started seeping onto Instagram. Photos like one of a prepubescent lady with a face she didn't grow herself, in pastel activewear, sipping a black-and-green health drink on a yacht on the French Riviera with the caption "School drop-off can be such a drag. #mumlife #blessed #whyme" were starting to make their way in between the everyday candid shots of friends' kids and three-legged dogs.

Hang on a minute! That isn't what drop-off looks like, is it? Oh shit, is it?

Then I started seeing people I know and love filter and crop their images to the point where I had to check the username to identify whose photos I was looking at.

Now, don't get me wrong, I love *some* editorial photos—you know, the ones where incredible supermodels are wearing clothes that only they are allowed to wear, and are on top of a building on a motorbike, with gimp masks on and shaved heads and nipple tassels, selling us the new empowering fragrance from YSL or DKNY or ABC. Yeah, *those* ones, the ones everyone knows are ridiculous and unattainable. The ones that only one type of lady is allowed to be a part of. The ones that make us have a moment of, "Oh fuck, is that how I should look if I want to be in a gimp mask on a motorbike on a roof?" Yes. The answer is yes, that is how you need to look to be a part of this ridiculous shit.

It has taken us years to get to this place of realizing that is bullshit and flat-out body shaming, so we can put down the magazine and move on with our day, without anyone getting too upset or confused. Even the models, the photographers, and the brand know what they are doing: showing us what we are not allowed to have and can't afford.

Some people love it, some people hate it, but we all know what it is. Unattainable. Fake.

That's fine. As I said, I think there is a place for these sorts of editorial photos. I could even go as far as to say that that is art. This stuff doesn't confuse or upset me anymore; it just makes bread taste even better.

Then Instagram came along, and all of a sudden we were meant to believe the French Riviera school mum is just the ordinary, the mundane, the norm? But surely we know that's not real, right? RIGHT?! Turns out these pastel-wearing Instagrammers—predominantly women—were making a fucking killing by tapping into a whole new world of insecurities that a lot of us didn't even know we had until we were scrolling through someone's feed at 3:00 a.m., regretting every life decision we had ever made.

I'm Starting Something

I love making fun of myself. The only other person in the world who loves it as much as I do is my sister, Olivia. We used to screenshot photos and send them to each other, challenging one another to have a go at imitating them.

The first #celestechallengeaccepted photo I did was easy. It was a lady doing a weird yoga pose up against a stairwell. I posted it to my Instagram page as well as my private Facebook page (I didn't have a public Facebook page at that point—I didn't need one, as I was managing my eighty-seven friends rather well) with the caption "I'm starting something." People liked it—*my* people liked it—and I got some fun comments and that was it. I went on this way for a few weeks, posting different photos—some on the beach, some in the bathroom, most of them featuring me scantily clad. It was fun. I knew it was funny, and people started to get on board.

Within a week I had gained around two thousand followers, and I was still having fun. Then I got a private Facebook message one day from someone at ABC Online, saying they would like to interview me about my take on social media. I had just posted my take on a photo of Kim Kardashian lying on a dirt hill in her underwear—BREAKING NEWS: that shoot was styled by her husband, Kanye—so I was happy to talk about my comedy and Kanye's "creative genius."

We did the interview, and the day after it was published, my following grew to about five thousand followers!

Five thousand followers! Holy shit! I'm no longer parodying Kim "Kimbo" Kardashian; I AM HER!

I instantly started to feel myself change, and I began deleting the numbers in my phone of people I thought were holding me back. I'm an Instagram sensation, goddamn it! I will only have positive people around me at all times, and I don't want any negativity, you guys.

That weekend our friends Kate and Phil came to stay for a few nights. They are two of our oldest friends, and when we all get together it's a boozefest. There's a lot of backslapping that goes on between Api and Phil, and Kate and I usually just sit and watch TV together, vowing never to talk or leave.

We had all assumed our respective positions of backslapping and idiot-box watching, all done with phones in hand of course, when we started getting messages from people via FB, Insta, pigeon, and fax that I was "blowing up."

The credible and always factual *Daily Mail* had taken the ABC Online article, totally butchered it, given no credit whatsoever to ABC Online, and published a story about me on their main page. I ain't got no loyalty—butcher that story, make shit up, say I've got forty-eight legs for all I care. I know the truth. You can't touch me, *Daily Mail*—just get me followers and MAKE ME FAMOUS!

And with that my following jumped by tens of thousands every few minutes.

Phil, the leader of the pack—well, he's the loudest, so he's the leader—invented a drinking game. All four of us sat around our dining table with our alcoholic beverages and were instructed by Phil to turn our phones onto airplane mode for one minute. Kate put a timer on. At this point I was at around eight thousand followers.

Phil announced that if in one minute I had gotten over ten thousand followers, we had to skull our drinks. We all cheered and thought what a bloody fun guy Phil was.

A minute later Kate's alarm went off; we all busted a nut to see who could reactivate their phone the fastest, and BAM, I was at fifteen thousand followers.

When we woke up the next morning with pretty sore heads, I had something like fifty thousand followers and about as many emails from my agent with interview requests.

After that night it just grew and grew and I got busier and busier, and a whole new world of seeing people getting paid for the most ridiculous things was in front of me.

Who Gives a Shit?

When I do interviews I will have to talk about what I do. "Oh, she's famous on Instagram," people will say to the makeup artist. Who cares, right? Because if you need to tell someone you're famous, you're not, in fact, famous.

Let me break down my tried-and-tested theory for you. Take Madonna and Beyoncé, for example (because all good theories start with Madonna and Beyoncé). I doubt during their first encounter at some super-fantastic, organic-wine, security-dressed-as-peacocks event that their publicists had to do introductions.

"Um, excuse me, Beyoncé, this is Madonna. She is a singer who is constantly reinventing her image and likes to push the boundaries of musical and cultural content. Oh, and she's the Queen of Pop. And Madonna, this is Beyoncé Knowles, but the world knows her as Bey. She is the founding member of '90s pop group Destiny's Child, has become the voice of women's empowerment, and makes us feel OK if we have a bit of junk in the trunk. She is Queen B." No, it didn't happen because it didn't need to, because these women are *famous*.

This may come as a rude shock to you, but I'm not in the same league as these ladies. I have, however, started to do famous-people stuff—interviews, openings—and it's fun, until I have to talk about me and why the hell I'm there.

If I'm getting my makeup done (fancy) for a TV interview, and the makeup artist asks why I'm there, my response is always a little, "Um, my Instagram account."

Makeup Artist: Really? What do you do with your Instagram account?

Me: Well, I take half-naked, inappropriate, and at times unflattering photos of myself.

MA: Really? That's why you're here?

Me: Um, yep. I'm also a comedian and an actor and about to tour America with—

Nup, they have already drowned me out with the hair dryer.

The interesting thing is that I've been acting on television for the best part of a decade and no one is interested, yet I posted one "Kim Kardashian on a dirt pile" photo and BAM, I'm running for president.

I've found myself in a number of situations where, to my embarrassment, I'm defending my Insta fame. People always say that money and fame can change you, and they advise you to keep your good friends close and listen to your family.

I'm not sure I totally agree with this. It turns out the friends I've had forever are the ones who are changing and trying to sell me out; *I'm* the one who has stayed normal, while these old school losers are proving to be dirty big-fame whores.

Some people I love have gone a bit crazy and are introducing me as "my mate Celeste; she's famous on Instagram." And before my new acquaintance can do the "oh, I guess I should care about this information" face, I want to scream at the top of my lungs "WHO GIVES A SHIT?" Because at the end of the day Instagram fame is not real-life fame/success. It's like when you think someone has shit dress sense and they tell you they like your outfit. It doesn't matter.

The One Where I Go to America

In 2016, after becoming an overnight success (eye roll emoji), I had some interest from a few managers and agencies over in America, and I wanted to get there and test the waters (which is college talk for binge on Shake Shack and write it off as a business trip).

When Lisa, my Australian agent—I've wanted to work with her since graduating from drama school in 2002, yet she only signed me three years ago (whatever)—told me that there were a few managers in America who wanted to meet with me I thought, "YES! I'm going to be on the reboot of *Friends*, or at the very least get to do the *Sex and the City* tour."

It was only a two-week trip, and since Api hadn't been to America before we decided to go over without the kids, as it would be too far for them and I'd be super busy shooting scenes with Lisa Kudrow. So we dropped them at my mum and dad's with a toothbrush and some broken memories and headed to the United States of America, the land of hopes, dreams, and an irrational need for cheese that comes out of a sauce bottle.

Before I had even met with my now US managers, they had already set up meetings with some pretty exciting people, people I never dreamed would want to meet with me. Later I learned that this was a technique to "get me." In America, if a manager is keen for you to work with them, they dazzle you with their bedazzled bits until you are blinded by all the pretty things and go with them.

In my experience, Americans in the entertainment industry are an energetic bunch. They are just as energetic about things they are excited about as they are about things that piss them off. This is the complete opposite of my experience with EVERYONE IN THE AUSTRALIAN ENTERTAINMENT INDUSTRY IN THE HISTORY OF THE WORLD!

In Australia, if someone thinks you're talented, you won't be called for a role, won't be pursued. You will feel as though you have been blacklisted by the industry, and when you talk to fellow acting friends in cafés about "why that casting agent didn't get you in for the role," all your friends get awkward and look away, compounding your feeling of being left out. You will write emails, get your agent to write emails, beg, borrow, and steal the audition piece so you can record the audition yourself—thinking this will make them like you, because you are completely doing their job for them—and send flowers, handwritten sonnets, and some illicit drugs to prove you are interested in the role, which you will hear nothing about. Then you will go to a party, where you will run into the uninterested manager/casting director/producer and learn that they think you are incredible, but the role has gone away because no one wanted to seem too interested.

I'm a hustler, so I love the American "you're hilarious" way of doing things. (NB If you think something is hilarious, *laugh*. I've encountered a lot of Americans who love *telling* me I'm hilarious but not actually *laughing* at any of my jokes. Is this a cultural thing, or do I need to work on new gags? Asking for a friend.)

When I got to America I was prepared. I didn't just go into meetings to shake hands and eat all the Mentos; I had show ideas and script ideas that I had had my agent send over before I had the meeting so we could talk about it.

And didn't we talk about it! Everything I said was met with "Wow!" or "You're hilarious!" The main catchphrase I had thrown at me was, "Oh God, we totally have a bunch of projects coming up here that you'd be PERFECT for," and I'm pretty sure in one meeting I was offered the gig of hosting the Oscars the following year.

Now, I'm no fool, especially in LA—it's a thing that I call "being LA-ed," where you are offered the world and nothing comes through. I know when people are blowing smoke up my arse, as it very rarely happens, because I make sure I surround myself with people who don't really let me get excited about much without a few "well, we can't all have fancy lunches with Rosie Huntington-Whiteley" comments, ensuring I stay grounded and not too big for myself.

But my situation was different. I'm not your average actor kicking it in LA. I'm funny, and I'm a big deal online (much like that monkey from *Friends*). I have a massive reach, so in the eyes of a network or producer I "come with an audience," which is very appealing (at least that's what I've been told).

Second and third meetings were being set up, and people wanted to see more of my stuff. I wasn't being LA-ed; *they* were being ceLAsted!*

Some of these meetings were with a bunch of geeky digital guys who were stoked to be able to talk about algorithms and were shocked to shit to learn that I do all my own stuff.

Stoked Digitalk Guy: OK, so who's your location scout?

Jet-Lagged Tech-Phobic Celeste: What do you mean?

SDG: Who do you employ to find the locations where you shoot the re-creations? Is it one guy, or do you have a team?

JTPC: A team? Are you kidding? I do it.

SDG: Really? You do it?

JTPC: Yep, it's not hard. If we're at the beach, I'll do some beach shots.

SDG: Yeah, right, cool. What about the captions? Does a freelance writer do those for you, or is it more of an in-house thing?

JTPC: Oh, it's definitely an in-house thing.

SDG: Sweet, so you and your team just spitball ideas, and then it gets rolling from there?

JTPC: Team? What the hell are you talking about? It's usually done while I'm cooking dinner and finishing off a glass of wine. I'll think of something funny, then post it.

SDG: Wow, who's the phot—

JTPC: OK, it's me! It's all me! There's no "team." It's me with the idea, me with the concept, me with the words, me with the gags, and then my husband takes the photo, and if he's not around, I get a friend to. But it's all me!

SDG: Wow, that's intense.

There are a lot of us Aussies in LA. We are everywhere. I have a heap of friends who have been over there for a while; some of them are killing it, while others are still working at it. Both situations work for me, as those in the former category invite me to fun stuff, and those in the latter category usually have a spare room because their parents need to fly over intermittently to comfort them while they wait tables and teach Pilates to cats. It also works because I have an instant family whenever I go over there—people to talk to about meetings, what cat Pilates is really like, and whether I should tip the valet's wife.

When you're in a town that's all about the Biz, it becomes all you talk about. And I love it. I can see how when you live there, talking "shop" all the time can be trying, but I don't live there, and the only reason I was there this time round was to get into the Biz, so I was chewing off friends' ears left, right, and center about the meetings I'd just had.

It's a good thing I do this, because after about thirty-four vodkas and twenty-three trips through the In-N-Out Burger drive-through, my mates assure me that I have in fact been LA-ed and that I should stop calling designers to get an Oscars frock because that shit ain't gonna happen. Damn you, jaded friends!

Soho House

The first place I met my future managers was at the Soho House West Hollywood. Think *Eyes Wide Shut* with less nudity and more Scientology. It was a midafternoon meeting that had been scheduled by about fifteen assistants who all went by the names of Peter, Steve, Carrie, or Sport.

Given it was a day meeting, and I'm all about my personality, I didn't think I needed to get too dressed up. Silly little hick girl. To the rest of the world, the Oscars are the fanciest event on everyone's calendar—well, that and that random gum boot–throwing competition they hold in New Zealand every year. Oh, no, my friends, the Oscars aren't fancy at all; it's just another Wednesday in Hollywood, because it seems that IN LA EVERYONE GETS DRESSED UP ALL THE TIME. The only people who don't get dressed up are the ones who wear activewear that costs more than my house.

I like looking good, but I don't like dressing up (until I put on an Alex Perry dress and realized that I'm much better when I can't breathe in couture). It also proves my mother's point that I'm afraid to look good. I was jet-lagged up to my tits, and my drinks hadn't kicked in yet, so I decided a cutoff denim skirt and some sort of ill-fitting black top thing was the right outfit for the occasion; it screamed cool, casual Instagram sensation, who is trained in the craft of acting, knows her shit, and has her #metoo stories ready to go at any given time.

This outfit was coupled with some pink Converses, and I immediately looked like I was a middle-aged ball girl at Wimbledon, a look that I still enjoy to this day. I'm a sneakers girl; I don't do heels. I mean, I LOVE high heels, but I can't *do* them. The only time I can commit to heels is if I'm being driven in a large car that allows me the room to place my feet over my head. I then get straight out of the car and take five assisted steps to the restaurant, where I can sit the entire time and it's socially acceptable for me to visit the ladies' room barefoot. Then after the meal and a gentle foot rub under the table, I can be carried to an awaiting car and whisked away. Only under these conditions will I strap my feet in all the Band-Aids available in the Southern Hemisphere, have a Valium, and pop on a pump. But as we know, these situations are only reserved for people whose names start and end with the letter *X.*

Soho House West Hollywood is for creatives, artists, people who need a space to be creative, productive, and seen.

There are two types of people who frequent these places:

People who aren't willing to be who they are, so they cut and crop themselves and wrap themselves up in really expensive cheap-looking skin and hide away from any adult responsibility, like paying your bills or wearing socks.

The ones who are so "real" and "normal" that every second word is "authentic" or "passion," and most sentences begin with "I'm just all about living my truth" or "the vibe in my head is so hectic right now," and they only hang around people they grew up with in a tiny town out the back of Bumfuck, Idaho, yet haven't seen in twenty-five years.

Soho House West Hollywood is on the top floor of the building, and you can access it only through a parking garage . Now, this may sound fancy, and it kind of is: people drive their self-driving spaceship cars into the secret underground parking garage, and in the middle of all the parking spots is a lobby, a beautiful room filled with even more beautiful, similar-looking people and warm lighting and the smell of money. Only this fancy spaceship parking garage isn't exclusively for Soho House show ponies—I mean writers—it's also a common parking garage where at any time Mariah Carey could get run over by someone in a not-so-fancy car while trying to reboot her career.

When I arrived, I regretted my outfit immediately. Scary Spice was wearing platform heels, an electric-blue onesie, and some sort of tiara and was yelling at the valet for not cleaning her car. It was SO exciting. I don't think she was annoyed, I just think this is how people in LA talk to people who do things for them.

You can't just go there for a cheeky afternoon spritzer. Oh, no, my silly little nonmember friends—one must be invited to Soho House by a member, and if you happen to arrive there before said member, you must sit in the gas-fumed lobby waiting for the member to be notified of your arrival. Then you are given directions to the fancy table areas, to be put on display—I mean, work on a script. It's so exclusive and fancy that you aren't even allowed to take photos.

So, just to unpack that for you, it's a members-only club in West Hollywood that only attractive, creative people are allowed to frequent and where no photos can be taken to prove that you were at an exclusive members-only club in West Hollywood with all the attractive, creative people like Lindsay Lohan's mum.

As soon as I got to the bar I felt instantly out of place, and that was fine. Being out of place in these sorts of places energizes me. It's weird. I guess not putting on a show but just relaxing with a thirty-five-dollar vodka gives me room to do what I want—stare at the pretty people, write jokes, and pick my nails.

There's a special place in there where you can take selfies that I'm pretty sure is called the Weinstein Booth. BUT THAT'S THE ONLY PLACE WHERE PHOTOS CAN BE TAKEN.

Of course, I didn't know this, so when I was about thirteen vodkas deep I decided I wanted to show my shit off to my sister, who was back in Brisbane doing important things like saving lives, so I sat at the lobby bar alone taking 986,824 photos of myself. A surprised face is the LA uniform, so I didn't worry when people started looking at me with surprised faces. But then I realized I was so not cool that I'd become cool, and it wasn't until I met with my would-be managers that I realized I couldn't take photos.

In between taking illegal selfies, I texted one of my would-be managers saying I was there. He responded, saying they were on the balcony and they would come and get me.

I skulled my vodka and sent a text: I'm in the bar, looking out of place.

He texted back immediately: Oh yeah, I can see you. I knew we would get along.

When I met my managers I started laughing.

Trevor is Mr. LA. He's a member of Soho House; in fact, he's there more often than the concierge. When we first met, he was fitting our meeting in between dates, and he also may or may not be the former husband of Mrs. Prince Harry! (SHUT UP!) And Steve is a comedy guy from New York who now lives in LA but is working as hard as he can to keep his NYC edge. He doesn't have any known ties to the monarchy.

I met with a lot of managers when I got to America, and these two were the most keen and excited about me. Whenever I told a joke, Trevor would drop his LA-dude persona, throw his head back, and laugh like a hyena, while Steve sniggered and took notes.

And neither of them *says* my jokes are funny; they just laugh.

I don't ever remember officially signing with these guys, but I'm not working with any other American managers at the moment, and these guys seem to be calling me the most, and I really like them. Something I've learned about LA is that the people in the Biz really rely on the idea "out of sight, out of mind." When I'm there I'm absolutely everywhere, but when I'm not around most of our conversations revolve around the comment, "Well, we can't wait to get you back out here," or "When are you planning on coming back out here?" or "Have you gained weight? In your Instagram photos you look like you've gained weight." (This isn't from my managers; this is from other random "Biz" folk.)

Ideally I'd like to "Hemsworth" it. I want to live in Australia and fly first class to America to work work work, then come back and watch my husband do sit-ups on the beach. I'm currently more like the brothers from the '90s band Hanson, trying to get people to take me seriously and asking people to pay for my lifestyle. Baby steps.

And, yes, I think I *have* gained weight.

The One When Harry Met Celeste

Another reason for heading to America was to meet Harry Connick Jr., as he wanted to have me on his show as a guest to talk about my Instagram account.

I remember when the call came through. I was SO excited! Harry Connick Jr. wanted me on the premiere week of his daytime talk show *Harry*! Holy shit, I mean he's no Ellen, but you know, beggars can't be choosers.

The show is filmed in New York. I LOVE New York. I have traveled there about five times in my life. The first time was when I was a kid and used to carry my teddy bear Sigmund around in my backpack with his head sticking out the top so he could see things that I couldn't, and we could recap that night in the hotel room in a bed that I had to share with my sister and her highly contagious chicken pox. The second time I went over was for a low-budget Australian film, *Burke & Wills*, in which I played the pivotal role of a character who had a one-night stand and was so memorable that the character's name was "Woman Who Has One-Night Stand." The film was accepted into the Tribeca Film Festival in 2006, and like any hustler who knows how to overstay her welcome, I booked myself a flight to the Big Apple and accompanied the director, who was pretty sure I was an extra in the film and was just over there for my birthday, and it was all just a coincidence.

I've also been a few times with friends and a number of times on my own, when I did some really stupid shit and can't believe that none of it has caught up with me yet (fingers crossed emoji).

But this was my first trip to New York for work, and my first with Api.

I've never known anyone to throw themselves into their hobbies quite like this man.

Above all, Api is a beach guy. He loves the water; if he hasn't been in it for a few days, he becomes really hard work. Every time he surfs he does it with such love and excitement it's as though he will never surf again—good way to live, right? Whenever we plan family holidays they always need to be on some sort of island so he can get in some waves. No complaints here—any excuse to squeeze this body into a bikini is a good vacay to me, amiright ladiezzz?!?!

So I was a little worried when Harry called and wanted us to go to New York City. There's surf in LA, but there ain't no surf breaks in New York City—not even from when that amazing pilot that Tom Hanks played in that movie landed on the Hudson: not wavy enough. But Api was stoked. He's a researcher not by trade, just by eagerness, so he googled every specialty skate shop and ramen house in the tri-state area. (I don't know what tri-state area means, but I hear it when people are referring to people looking really hard for things, so there it is.)

We were put up in a hotel room in New York, and it was everything you could hope and wish for when being put up by a fancy television network. The foyer was amazing; it had massive chandeliers hanging from the ceiling and doorways, a huge vine was wrapped all over every-thing, and when we walked up the amazing dark wooden staircase, rich, polite people smiled and the vine even tried to grow over my face. It was so fancy that after we had checked in and been given our room keys, I had to double-check with the concierge that we were in the right place.

We walked through the beautiful halls of the thirteenth floor. The carpet wasn't sticky, which was a nice change from the New York hotel I usually stay in, and the walls were a beautiful tone of "cash and class." Api and I were out of place, and we bloody loved it.

The bellboy (is that what they are called, or am I being racist?) who was carrying our two bags and three new skateboards swiped the card to open the door to our room. He opened the door for us only partly, and with a smile handed us the room key and told us to enjoy our stay, and with that he disappeared.

Api grabbed our luggage, and I attempted to open the door farther to let the precious cargo through. I quickly realized this was as far as the door would open, as it was banging into the bathroom wall.

We squeezed into the room and discovered there was only enough room for one adult and a teacup Chihuahua. The room comprised a double bed, a bathroom housing half a shower, and a safe. We spent the following three nights in the hotel with the fancy foyer sleeping with our two suitcases and three skateboards in bed with us.

The morning of the *Harry* show I had my game face on. I was pimply, bloated, and jet-lagged like a bitch, but I was ready, goddamn it. Api *needed* to see a skate shop downtown, and there was no way on God's green earth I was going to go with him; I had a date with Harry. I sat in the shoebox-inside-the-shoebox-size room and got focused.

Api got home from Skate City about ten minutes before we needed to leave and somehow in seven minutes managed to shit, shower, and shave and come out looking and smelling like Taye Diggs and the Rock had had a baby (I'll just leave that image there).

We walked to the studio from where we were staying because we were in New York City, baby, and that's what you do—you walk.

As soon as we got to the studio, I was "on." People like to think that actors are always on; trust me, we're not. Only yesterday did my children have to drag me out of bed at 11:00 a.m. because I was having a prolonged moment of sadness and couldn't get out of my own way (everyone calm down, it was a Sunday—no one was missing any school).

A lot of actors and comedians I know don't like being the center of attention. That's not the case with me.

Most actors and comedians LOVE to work, and even though entertaining people in the line at Kmart when you've run in ten minutes before school starts to pick up a pair of shoes because your seven-year-old always loses his left shoe might be hard work at times, it's not the type of work I mean. Being "on" when I'm not prepared for it gives me anxiety and is really exhausting. But when I'm at work and feeling good and at the top of my game, then I'm on, oh I'm on like *Donkey Kong*!

When we arrived at the studio, I gave them my name at reception and they knew who I was!

This was massive for me. I'm the type of person who will introduce myself to you over and over again because I'm sure you have forgotten me. I reintroduced myself to one of my bridesmaids on my wedding day.

We were shown to a dressing room by a lovely lady who was a bit of a fan of Australian television and was "obsessed with *All Saints*, and never missed an episode," yet she couldn't recall me at all.

My dressing room was filled with treats, which as soon as no one was looking Api and I stashed in my bag for after-show celebratory snacks. Then it was off to the Makeup Room, and this is where I come alive.

You know those warm-up guys who come out before a talk show and warm up the audience? They have a set number of jokes that everyone has heard before but still loves—"Hey, where are you from?" "Brisbane." "Sorry." "BRISBANE!" the audience member yells, thinking they can't be heard. "No, I heard you, I'm just sorry"—all the best gags. Everybody laughs, there's some knee slapping that happens, and everyone forgets their troubles.

Well, I'm that guy when I get into Hair and Makeup. When I walk into the Makeup Room, I want to shake shit up. I read the room, completely disregard what I've read, then just go at it. It's not a contrived thing; it's just what feels right. Makeup Rooms are usually filled with sassy young women, a few queens, and the odd middle-aged woman who didn't think she would still be doing this at her age, and it's where I come alive. I thank Jo for this—whenever I walked into her Makeup Room, she would look at me with a big smile, already laughing at something I was going to say while setting up her makeup station.

My go-to joke as soon as I walk in, with no makeup, bags under my eyes, my hair usually wet, and a questionable lump on my nose, is: "Actually, you guys, I'm good to go. I don't need any hair or makeup today, just maybe a clear gloss on my lips, but nothing more."

There is usually a pause, the hair and makeup artists look at each other a little confused, then we all laugh at what a crazy gal I am. This is my icebreaker; it helps me get into the vibe. Api says he loves watching me "get into character," or get into the space, and it all starts in Hair and Makeup.

Hair and makeup artists are the most knowledgeable people in the world. If you are ever looking to see a shrink or a psychiatrist, check to see if they were a hair or makeup artist in a former life and you will know they have heard it all before and you are in safe hands. I become friends with all the people who do my face and hair, not only because I'm a charitable person, but because these people get to know more about me than anyone, and as they say, keep your friends close and enemies closer.

You sit in their chair whinging about your marriage with morning breath and head lice, while they touch your face and sort out your earwax at 5:00 a.m. These people own you. And they pop up everywhere. They are the first people you see at work, the last people you see at the end of a day offering you makeup wipes, and the only ones you want to see in bed with you after a massive wrap party.

They are there just before you "go on," doing touch-ups or "checks," as it's called in the Biz; they are there at lunch watching you inhale all the pasta to make sure it doesn't smudge your lips; they even have control over how hydrated you are. These people are your FAM!

Before the *Harry* show, a fabulous Hispanic man touched my face in all the right ways in the makeup chair; then I moved over to another area of the huge Makeup Room (it was about 45,464 times bigger than our room at our hotel), where an amazing black lady with the most incredible earrings did things to my hair that only an amazing black lady with incredible earrings could.

After forty-five minutes of me trying out new gags and us all laughing and exchanging details, I exited my Hair and Makeup mecca, waved goodbye to my new adopted fam bam, and knew it wouldn't be long before I saw them again.

Then it was time to meet Harry, and I was ready. I was excited and cool and energized—all the things that Api wasn't. He was petrified.

Sorry, I'm not sure if I've made it clear: it was a *solo* interview, just me and my new mate from the South, Harry. Api had just come along for the ride, a ride that I wasn't interested in taking without him, but the interview, the actual reason we were there, was just for Harry and Celeste. Yet Api was acting as though we had just got word that Harry had fallen ill and he, Apihana Les Robin, the little Maori boy from the South Coast of New South Wales, had to take the reins and host the show, shirtless, while tap-dancing and speaking Swahili.

But no, he was just required to hang with me backstage and look good. I guess if I'd wanted some water or something and there wasn't enough time for me to get it, I could have asked him, but there are usually people who do this for you, so he just needed to stand near a wall and "enjoy."

By this point he was flat out just standing. He was tripping over cables, running into people, and once he finally thought he was all good and had found himself a spot to see what was going on but also be out of the way, he realized he was in a doorway that a massive coffee table had to be ushered through, forcing him to move and starting the tripping, stumbling cycle all over again.

We stood side stage for a while as Harry finished up with the guest who was on before me, my Hair and Makeup fam bam came over to do one last poke and prod, then it was on. I walked out to the small platform where I would be sitting, said hi to the studio audience, and took my seat.

In those situations no one really cares about what the guest is doing, as all people in the studio audience want to see is what goes on behind the scenes of a talk show and what the host does when they aren't "on."

I went to a taping of *Ellen* in 2010, and this was all I was interested in. For some reason I thought that the host hung out and chatted to the audience, but they don't—they're busy and need to prep for the next segment. During a break in the taping two security guards would come out and stand either side of Ellen while her Hair and Makeup fam bam fussed over her and one producer talked to her while another one showed her her cue cards and what she needed to do for the next segment.

It was the best theater I had ever watched. Minnie Driver and Perez Hilton were guests on *Ellen* for the episode we watched the taping of (remember, it was 2010), and I've never cared less about Minnie Driver in my life—and that's saying a lot, because *Good Will Hunting* is one of my favorite films. It was all eyes on Ellen.

Watching people when they aren't "on" is my favorite pastime. I'm that person at the train station watching a mother mumble "for fuck's sake" under her breath when her toddler asks for another rice cracker.

I felt I was prepared for the interview; the only thing that seemed to catch me off guard was the fact that I didn't walk out to the stage when introduced. Instead, I was already seated, with Harry standing in front of me.

When we got the countdown to come back from the ad break, I realized that I was, in fact, sitting, and didn't know if I needed to stand for the introduction, allowing me to greet Harry properly with a hug and kiss, after which we would sit down together and proceed with the interview, which would go viral, attracting twenty million Facebook views in the first three minutes. So I decided to sit for the introduction and planned that when Harry had finished the intro, in the time he took to turn around and walk two steps over to me, I would jump up and hug and kiss him, and the internet-breaking interview would be underway.

Instead of this flawless plan playing out, I realized that the plastic-coated jeans I was wearing were about two sizes too small and the type of jeans that need a solid fifteen minutes of adjustments once you were seated in position, and once adjusted they wouldn't allow the kind of swift movement I was planning on.

The next thing I hear is, "And we're back in three, two . . ."

Silence. Then the dreamy Harry Connick Jr., with his even dreamier southern twang, began: "My next guest is an Australian actor, comedian . . ." while all I can think is, "Shit, I don't have time to move!"

I now realized why Api was so worried. By the time Harry had spun around to greet me, I could tell my plastic-coated pants were hanging on by a thread.

"This is my first international talk show, goddamn it," I told myself. "I'm not going to let some ill-fitting pants prevent me from hugging Harry Connick Jr."

My pants had other things in mind. They had stuck themselves to me in the way a toddler sticks itself to an emptying breast, and they didn't let me move.

I managed to lean forward slightly, then in a moment of mercy my pants seemed to slingshot me into Harry's arms, and my teeth landed aggressively on his shoulder. There were about six cameras on us the whole interview, but the only photo I have of us is the one where I'm not quite standing and not quite sitting, rather half clutching Harry for dear life.

And that, my friends, is why my husband was a basket case leading up to the show.

The One Where I Become an #accidental(role)model

I have a really full-on love affair with women. I think women as a species are fucking incredible. We are excellent, we really are. Serena Williams winning a grand slam at twenty weeks pregnant? Give me a break. Oprah's Golden Globes speech? Sheesh. Malala Yousafzai and her humanitarian work, especially in women's and girls' education? Shut up already! The divine Rosie Batty showing incredible strength through such grief at losing her boy at the hands of his father and educating us on the meaning of love and resilience? POWERFUL. And of course the great Tina Fey calling the Nazis at the Charlottesville riots "chinless turds." I'M DONE!

Women are the tits.

I'm a girl's girl. If I'm in a group of women, I'll talk about everything from the pay gap to the possibility of a third *Sex and the City* movie, and before I leave I'll inevitably find out everyone's #metoo story (sad face emoji). This obviously doesn't happen when I'm in a group of gay men, because why would I ever leave a group of gay men for anything ever? Except, maybe, for a group of drag queens, with ice cream and a hat.

I'm all about the sisterhood, the Girl Code. "Colors of the world! Spice up your life! Every boy and every girl! Spice up your life! People of the world! Spice up your life! AHHHHHH!" Sing it, queens! (Or just let us remember you singing it, because the thought of the Spice Girls reforming scares me no end.)

We ladies need to focus on equal pay, equal rights, equal opportunity, equal equality. This, as a feminist, is what *I* focus on. It's not only important—it's vital.

But I take issue with being told *all* women should support each other. I don't buy into the idea that we women aren't allowed to *not* like one another just because we are women.

Before you unfollow me and go and burn my overpriced merch, let me explain.

If I don't like what you are doing, if you are making a living off belittling other people, other women, and making them feel like shit about how they look, or pushing a shitty agenda about mothering standards, then I'm not going to support you just because we both have a vagina.

If you are a bit shit to me or my mates and you happen to be a female, I'm probs not going to be your biggest fan just because we share the "luxury" of buying tampons.

Because sometimes, some people who happen to be women can be shit. They can body shame us and make us believe it is empowering, and if we don't agree with them, then we are antifeminist and are accused of not being supportive of our fellow sisters.

I agree that women need to support each other, and there is room for us all, but I think it's really important to remember that not all women have to love all women just because we are, in fact, all women. And to me, *that* is feminism.

I'm a feminist in every sense of the word. I support women, I fantasize about dyeing my hair pink (but due to lack of jaw definition I just don't think it would work), I march, I watch all-women comedy specials, and I think we deserve the same as men. I support women I want to support, and I call bullshit on women I think need to be called bullshit on, and that to me is feminism.

Judging someone on their worth, their character, their merit, not on the fact that they also struggle with underwire, that's feminism. If a lady is being a bit shit, then I'm not going to love that lady just because we have the same genitals; I'm going to give her and myself enough respect to look past the similar bustline and read the message for what it is. I don't want "charity support" from no woman just because I'm a woman, and in turn no woman is going to get "charity support" from me.

Banding together because we have been told that is what we need to be doing as women is putting feminism back decades and is completely missing the point. In my experience, most women as individuals are incredible, and there are also some women who are a bit rubbish, and that's OK too.

This is part of the problem. If women were equal in society, we would then not be judged if we decided not to love a fellow sister because they were a bit of a dick.

The sentiment that all women need to support each other no matter what is evidence that we are *not* equal—yet.

Body Shaming Is Big Business And It's Everywhere!

I've never really put my back into dieting; it's never really been my thing. I'm not interested in any interaction, attention, or success built on how I look, but mainly because I like food too much. In my younger years I would sometimes set up camp, boil the kettle, log on to Netflix, and take up residence in hating my body, but I don't ever remember a time when I committed to only eating a certain way to look a certain way.

I'm the kind of lady who couldn't hide my love of food even if I wanted or was paid to. If I've been shame-eating too many Tim Tams, my double chins double in size and rat me out, though luckily I'm tall (think Victoria's Secret model), so the pint of cookies-and-cream ice cream I demolish in one sitting spreads itself out evenly over my lumps and bumps. #blessed.

I have the palate of a racist seven-year-old: if it's white and has sugar in it, it's mine, all mine, don't think I'll be sharing any with you, fool. I was *that* kid at school who would finish my kick-arse lunch, then sit next to someone else who had a kick-arse lunch and be their instant yet temporary BFF.

"I really like your lunchbox. Where did you get it from?" I would ask as my unsuspecting sugar daddy would get out his homemade choc chip muffin.

"I know what you're doing, Celeste," he would respond while rolling his eyes.

I would feign shock. "What?! I'm honestly wondering where your mum shops and where she buys such great compartmentalized plastic food containers that store your delicious food so efficiently."

"You can't have any of my muffin."

"Wha—why would you think I was just here to have a taste of your amazing, freshly baked muffin?"

"Because I heard you say to Stacy that you're going to come over here and try to steal some of my muffin."

Fuck Stacy!

I don't think I'm great at diets because I don't care enough. I tried quitting sugar once. I dropped a heap of weight, a heap of purpose, and a heap of friends and wanted to punch a vegan.

I successfully yet unintentionally messed up intermittent fasting for a solid eight months. You know the diet where you stop eating at 7:00 p.m. and don't eat again until 10:00 a.m.? I got this mixed up and stopped eating at 10:00 p.m. and started eating again after 7:00 a.m., believing it was the easiest diet in the world! I would set an alarm at 6:45 a.m. to wake up and eat. That's how committed I was to it.

And I thought that the shake diet was fantastic. I would *add* a shake to my meals, as opposed to replacing the meal with the shake.

People think that looking the way I do is easy, or lazy, but I'm here to dispel those myths. Maintaining my look is a full-time job. I'm flat out remaining full; it's something that I work on all day, every day, and I really beat myself up if I go somewhere and am hungry and haven't come prepared with an apple and three peanut butter crumpets in a baggie. And maybe a Kit Kat, and a smoothie, maybe a hard-boiled egg.

After my heart surgery I was on crazy drugs for eight weeks that completely messed up my body and was advised to do a no-dairy, no-gluten, no-taste cleanse, coupled with a few enemas, to try to rid myself of the constipating drugs that had taken residence within me—nice.

At the time I felt like crap. Not only did I quit these food groups, but I also nearly quit #hothusband, my job, my dog, and my life. I knew, however, it was what was needed, and after what felt like a three-MILLION-week cleanse, I felt better. I don't think I looked much different, but I felt different. I felt healthy.

And herein lies the problem.

Feeling healthy and looking a certain way seem to be getting confused with each other.

Body shaming and healthy living aren't the same thing. They aren't Mary-Kate and Ashley Olsen. They aren't identical twins with a few cute and quirky differences, like they both enjoy wearing oversize clothes and marrying older men but as if one has a secret crack addiction that no one really cares about. No, they are different things, completely different ideals, and should be looked at as completely different industries.

Body Shaming is the mean football guy who drives around in his parents' Maserati, showing how important it is to make others feel inferior and making a fortune off it. It's the guy who gets all the ladies by showing them what he has and not risking any sort of genuine connection. The guy who bullies people into liking him, even though he's a douche, a mean guy who looks nice in an expensive three-piece suit.

I hate this guy. And this guy is EVERYWHERE. Popping up in the checkout line at the supermarket, pretending to be a supermodel who is hitting back at people who don't agree with everything he says. He's at the beach, in the toilet at the fancy restaurant, and blinding my eyes at 3:00 a.m. when I can't sleep and want to scroll through cute photos of dogs dancing. He's fucking everywhere.

Then there's the Healthy Living Guy. He's the quiet guy, the fair guy, the guy who hangs out in the drama room devising different ways to make people laugh. The guy who does Body Shaming Guy's homework and is fine with him getting all the credit. He's the guy who works two jobs after school to help out his parents. The one who has ideas about what might make you feel better about yourself but won't cut you off and bitch about you to Body Shaming Guy if you don't take his advice.

#istandwithhealthylivingguy.

Body Shaming Guy needs to stop going around to Healthy Living Guy's place, breaking in at night, going through his wardrobe, dressing up in his clothes, and pretending to be there for you. You're not welcome, Body Shaming Guy!

I'm not against looking good, fit, amazing, tight, small, muscly, great, whatever throws your hair back. But there is a multibillion-dollar machine supporting this at-times dangerous way of life, and that is a machine that is getting out of control. People—gorgeous people, genetically blessed people, privileged people, and at times unhealthy people—have all of a sudden become "experts" and the moral guardians of how we should be treating ourselves and our bodies.

Now, one might be forgiven for thinking that they are experts on healthy living and body image because they know how to tackle a catwalk or what angle one should hold one's head at for the perfect photo, but, my faithful, optimistic friends, they aren't. Instead they are giving us made-up advice on our health and how we should or, more to the point, shouldn't look.

Magazines get all excited when a supermodel is going to be a guest editor, weighing in (pardon the pun) on what we should be eating to get our body beach ready and giving us five quick tips on getting a box gap.

When Ashley Graham is interviewed she is introduced as a plus-size model, and a lot of the time her weight is a talking point, because we are conditioned to think that a woman who doesn't fit the beauty standards is not normal. She's not healthy—she's an exception. You very rarely see a *regular* model being interviewed and asked about her weight, because the modeling industry is what people are now expected to believe is normal, healthy, everyday, and attainable.

Body Shaming Is Taking Over the World

Holy shit, I love some bloody Super Bowl halftime entertainment. I love it. I love the buildup, I love how full-on people are about it, I love how much money is wasted, ahem, spent on it. I love it. It's always a weird mash-up of past musicians trying to stay relevant and current entertainers trying to prove they know what integrity is. In 2014 Bruno Mars and the Red Hot Chili Peppers rocked out, and the fact that Flea hasn't gotten whiplash after all these years still astounds me. In 2013 Beyoncé reunited with her Destiny's Child bandmates Kelly Rowland and "the Other One" to deliver a stellar performance; a bit of bloody Madge hit the stage in 2012; Katy Perry's nana dancing with Missy Elliott and a shark in 2015 was equal parts entertaining and awkward; and no one can forget Janet Jackson's nipple in 2004—I've been told that Justin Timberlake performed with her, yet I can't be sure.

And in 2017 at the fifty-first Super Bowl, it was Lady Gaga's turn, and didn't she smash it?!

If you're not a fan of sport and like me whinge and bitch every time your #hothusband wants to watch some "epic battle" instead of a recap of *The Real Housewives of Beverly Hills*, you may have looked online for the halftime show, sorry, PEPSI ZERO SUGAR SUPER BOWL HALFTIME SHOW, and you would be forgiven if you couldn't find the Gaga extravaganza straightaway.

Instead, the internet was full of comments, blogs, and columns telling us that Lady Gaga has a belly.

That's right, my friends, Lady Gaga—born Stefani Joanne Angelina Germanotta—has, in fact, got a stomach. I'm sorry, you guys. I should have put a warning at the beginning of this chapter advising y'all to sit down before reading that. It's a shock, I know, and I'm sorry for any offense caused. Jeez!

Also, THAT'S NOT A STOMACH.

I'm currently wearing my stepdaughter's activewear and not sure if I should choose a camel toe over a muffin top, as my belly situation is doing its best to fight back.

I like to pride myself on honesty, I really do. Very rarely are people unsure of where they stand with me. I don't think I'm rude; I'm honest. If I don't like something, I'll tell you. If I'm nervous, I'll fart. If I'm bored, I'll yawn (OK, maybe the yawning is a bit rude), but I do honesty, and I do it well.

See, I'm an actor by trade, so taking notes from people is part of the job—that and demanding that no one look me directly in the eyes after 4:00 p.m., and that my pants are always hand-washed in organic snail mucus.

Gaga looked banging at the Super Bowl, but I'm a little crazy and am from the school of thought that says resembling a malnourished praying mantis isn't a necessity to look good.

Her performance was super-duper. She sounded amazing, she jumped off a building, looking like a spider falling from the roof, she got weird with props, threw the microphone, caught a football, and did magic tricks in the form of costume changes that were not visible to the naked eye.

Yet all we were allowed to focus on was how she looked. Enough with the focus on the waistline of the tiny, fit, talented, kind of weird, super-quirky, trailblazing talent who was on a stage in front of more than 110 million people slaying her performance while still managing to say hi to her mum and dad!

And now the beach isn't off-limits either. Oh God, Mother Nature is being dragged into the body-shaming world kicking and screaming much like when Charlie Sheen was dragged into rehab.

Last time I checked, the beach was a place where the ocean meets the land. Where children frolic at the water's edge and manage to get sand in places only major organs belong. But not anymore; now it has become a fearful playground of insecurities, a melting pot of tight, brown (but not too brown), shaved, shiny, bendy bodies that look at dimply, saggy bodies as though the owners of those saggy bodies are one-legged dogs trying to climb a cactus.

Aren't we bored with this yet? I know *I* am. If looks were the main focus for men, then Trump would have been impeached the day after conception.[11]

---

11   Sorry.

The One about Loving Our Bodies #bopo

I have been told that I'm a contributor to the #bopo movement (for those of us over the age of six, #bopo is short for "body positive"). I've also been told that I should think before I speak and if I don't stop eating Tim Tams, I will develop type 2 diabetes, so I TAKE ALL THESE THINGS WITH A GRAIN OF SALT.

Much like Kim and Kayne get #kimye or Brad and Angelina got #brangelina or Celeste Barber and Beyoncé get #celyoncé (still trying to get this one off the ground), body positive got its own mash-up: #bopo. I'm totally into this and super excited to be a part of the #bopo movement. Well, I was until I googled it and found out the Urban Dictionary describes "bopo" as:

Beat Off, Pass Out: to masturbate aggressively to the point of exhaustive ejaculation and enjoying a heavy nap immediately after said self-pleasure.

Example 1:

Me: Looks like I have the afternoon off; think I might BOPO.

Example 2:

Student 1: This class blows. I stayed up all night doing that paper!

Student 2: Sounds like you could use some nice BOPO.

Student 1: No doubt, bro.

Example 3:

Taylor was upset to find her boyfriend, Austin, had already BOPO'd on the couch when she got home from work, because for once she didn't "have a headache."

I have been throwing around the hashie #bopo for ages now seeing as it has been thrown at me from so many directions, and because I played softball as a kid I'm good with throwing and catching. I never started the Instagram hashie #celestechallengeaccepted as a body positive thing. I just did it because I thought it was funny and I like making fun of myself; turns out most of you are happy with it too (grateful emoji).

I've been asked in a number of interviews how I'm going to get my body into shape for summer. To which I respond: "What shape are you referring to? I'm working on the wobbly pear shape at the moment and am quite happy with my progress." Crickets.

I strongly believe that how we look makes up a very small percentage of who we are. It's something that we as women, and I'm sure some men (though I can only talk for the ladies), have to remind ourselves of on a daily basis.

I think I look OK, I really do—yep, I'd like to have a smaller stomach, a more defined bum, and some serious Michelle Obama arms, but

I don't, and I'm OK with that. You know what I do have? A fucking excellent sense of humor, a heap of empathy for people who aren't feeling themselves, and bloody good legs.

As I write this I'm about to embark on an American tour of my live show #CelesteChallengeAccepted Live (yep, some of the greatest minds in the Biz came up with that fancy title), and I need to get fit. When I did my Australian tour I found out that I'm really *unfit*. I dance around onstage, I do a bit of unrehearsed floor work, and I run around like a chicken with no head. It's awesome, but I can't talk or keep up with my gags after a dance break, so I'm getting fit.

People who see me walking, or on very rare occasions running, have said to me, "Don't lose too much weight—you'll lose your audience."

I'm not doing these parody pics to show what it would look like for a fat girl to do a Kim Kardashian photo; I'm doing them because I think they are funny. I don't compare my body with the bodies of the people I parody. The first thing I think when I see a pic I want to parody is, "How would I look doing that?" Not "How fat would I look doing that?" or "How gross would I look doing that pose?" I simply ask myself, "Will that be funny if I do it?" If the answer is yes, then #hothusband is dragged out of the surf, and the three-minute photo shoot is underway.

I can't fit into my size 14 control pants. Look, I could look a lot better, or sexier (whatever that means), but I don't want to. I don't want to sacrifice eating cake at my son's birthday party (or on Wednesdays and Sundays), and I'm not about to pass on celebrating friends' successes with a glass of champagne just to fit an ideal. I have a real beef with an unattainable lifestyle being publicized as attainable and healthy. It's not healthy; it's one-dimensional. It's striving for one thing: not for strength, not for health, but to look good.

I think the idea of everything in moderation is a really good one. Maybe we could apply that idea to the bullshit we get fed about how we should all look.

There is so much talk about what we should and shouldn't look like and very little about how we are feeling. So instead of adding to the already noisy conversation with an InstaQuote of advice, I'm just going to get on with it—and if you need me, I'll be in the drama room writing some jokes that won't change the world but will hopefully make you laugh.

The One with My 28-Day Journey to Better Diet and Exercise

Week One

Morning

Wake up at 4:30 a.m., and before you've even put your feet on the ground you're already in your activewear and are sure you've lost weight because your attitude has changed.

Today is the start of the new you, so you need new everything—new kettle, new activewear, new blender, new clothesline, new journal, and new dining chairs. New new new. Before the kids are awake, head to the kitchen and boil the brand-new filtered water with the brand-new kettle you bought two days ago. While the water is boiling, juice your organic lemons in your new fancy juicer. As you sip on your hot lemon water, strap on your Fitbit and get ready to start counting your steps.

Make sure to note all the things you put in your mouth over the next twenty-eight days in your brand-new kikki.K food journal that you bought on sale. And scream at your children for even thinking of borrowing the matching pen. Log on to Instagram and start a new page, alerting your followers that you are going in a new direction with your posts and will be sharing your daily food intake and workouts with everyone to hold yourself accountable. You'll be posting about how fabulous you feel cutting out coffee and replacing it with herbal tea, and how all the clothes you kept from your Year 10 Janet Jackson days are now hanging in your wardrobe waiting to be worn.

Spend your month's wage when you sign up to a healthy living website, and be sure to jot down the first of many inspiring quotes you need to do to be a better, more attractive person.

Midmorning

Eat one of the 145 boiled eggs you prepared the day before, and drink five liters of water along with a peppermint tea, no honey.

After dropping the kids at school, go for your walk. Your Fitbit goal should be fifteen thousand, and you're determined to get the steps in before pickup. Because this is the new you. The healthy and skinny you. The REAL you.

Lunch

Slice an avocado in half as a bread substitute and place another boiled egg on top. Followed up by your sixth liter of water. Instead of addressing the dizzy spells, focus on the positives and journal about them.

Afternoon Tea

Consume no more than five activated almonds and a slice of raw salmon. Consume two liters of water and start judging other people.

Dinner

While watching your family enjoy the spaghetti Bolognese you prepared for them, full of cheese and pasta, take a teaspoon of Bolognese sauce and place it in a lettuce-leaf cup and remember how lucky you are, how skinny you're going to be, and how easy this way of living actually is.

After-Dinner Treat

A cup of herbal tea and a liter of water.

While sipping on your relaxing tea, log on and look at some more inspiring healthy living websites. You will fast realize that you are actually one of those people now and be proud to know that you have started on this new way of life, and as soon as you lose a lot of weight you'll be a better person.

Bedtime

Check your Fitbit and realize you have done 75K steps. Go to bed knowing you are amazing and can do anything and that wine doesn't really rule your life like it does the lives of all your friends.

Follow these steps for every day of Week One, and you'll be feeling tetchy and thin.

NB Around Day Two you will be feeling really fucking angry and in pain. Keep some Tylenol on you at all times, and for the after-dinner snack I suggest drinking your herbal tea from a wineglass to trick your brain.

Week Two

Morning

Even though you've fallen off the wagon a little since the first day of Week One, today is the day you're going to get back onto it. Start introducing things back into your diet, because after all, it's not a diet, you guys—it's a new way of living. Put on some ill-fitting pajama bottoms and your gym top that hasn't been washed since your stepdaughter wore it to her athletics carnival, and get ready for the day.

Midmorning

You have replaced the peppermint tea with a large soy latte and the boiled egg with scrambled eggs and a small piece of toast, and some bacon, for extra protein.

When you go to write in your food journal, you realize that due to a sugar, carb, and wine shortage, your blood sugar has plummeted and you have accidentally packed your food journal in your son's library bag and are staring at the cover of *Harry Potter and the Philosopher's Stone*. You don't worry, as you still have your new and improved Instagram account to help you stay accountable. While uploading a photo of your scrambled eggs, make sure you charge your Fitbit, which you forgot to do after taking it off last night when you went for cocktails with your girlfriends. One slipup is OK.

Lunch

You are too full from the midmorning snack of scrambled eggs, bacon, toast, and a sneaky bag of chips to eat anything for lunch, so you just get a banana smoothie, feeling good about having a liquid lunch.

Afternoon Tea

As you didn't technically "eat" lunch, you make up for the lost calories with some banana bread. Since you are still focused on your health and hydration, you skull a glass of water and two multivitamins.

Dinner

Still proud of skipping lunch, you celebrate with two glasses of wine and four of your kids' half-eaten fish fingers.

Bedtime

Try to skull four of the five liters of water you should have been sipping throughout the day while looking at '90s photos of Jennifer Aniston doing yoga, open a new browser page, and book yourself in for a Bikram yoga class in the morning.

Week Three

Morning

Wake up, remember you stayed up way too late last night watching *The Office* outtakes and forgot to set your alarm, and it's now 8:35 and you have done fuck all.

While ordering your kids' school lunch online, try to put some left-over lemon from last night's fried rice in scalding hot water and skull it in the hope that it will somehow cleanse the bottle of wine you've been consuming nightly since Day Two of Week Two.

Midmorning

You ran out of time at home to do anything with the eggs your husband keeps boiling and had to be at school by eight. Running late, you whip into the Macca's drive-through and order a Bacon 'N Egg McMuffin and remind yourself you are halfway through this new way of living, so you check yourself and order only one hash brown.

Lunch

Eat the leftover fried rice from dinner the night before and a protein shake to fill you up for the rest of the day.

Afternoon Tea

Log on to Instagram and realize that you may have slipped a little. Open another browser and realize the healthy living website you took down all the notes from is actually a body-shaming website. Go into your room and scream into a pillow until dinner.

Dinner

While cooking risotto (a family favorite and a personal favorite, as you can drink while cooking), you realize you have done only two thousand steps in the past four days and begin to run on the spot while cooking, drinking, and helping your children with their homework.

After-Dinner Snack

Shame-eat the risotto your children didn't finish in the kitchen pantry so no one can see you. Wash it down with five liters of vodka, lime, soda, and tears.

Week Four

Realizing you are better than this, call your best friend and organize an impromptu weekend away consisting of wine, caftans, *Will and Grace* binges, and all-you-can-eat buffets.

Week Forever

And give yourself a fucking break.

The One Where I Explain Why
I Don't Hate Hot People

I want to be clear about something. Something that I think people are a bit unsure of when they look at me or my "brand." I don't hate hot people. I really don't. I just get a bit annoyed that they seem to get away with things that not-so-hot people *don't* get away with.

The other day I was talking to #hothusband, and as I began opening up about my feelings and hopes and dreams, he just started yawning.

While he was mid-yawn, I stopped abruptly and asked: "Um, are you yawning?"

To which he responded, "I just get really tired when you start talking."

Now, if some guy who looked like Trump Jr.[12] had said that to me, he would have gotten a swift kick to the dick. I would have screamed at him and stormed off to my room and accessed my emergency stash of wine, nicely placed in my underwear drawer, under the bed, in my shoe drawer, or in the pot plant next to my bed.

But because #hothusband is such an Adonis, I found myself reassessing the way I was delivering him information. Thinking it was *me*

---

who was the problem, I figured I needed to come up with more exciting ways to engage with him.

But I don't hate hot people, I really don't. If anything, I'm concerned for them.

Have you noticed that most hot people you see in the street look confused? They are walking around looking for the perfect light, with a look on their faces of "Oh shit, I only came out this morning to show this face and/or body off; I've got no idea what to do with the rest of my life."

This is worrying. You never see an average-looking person looking confused in the street. We are busy and rude and have places to go so we can prove our worth, because fuck knows we didn't get where we are based on our faces alone.

Kate Beckinsale (hair flick emoji) commented on one of my photos the other day, to which #hothusband said, "Oh, she seems pretty cool." He then paused and said, "Oh, I know she's hot, but she still seems pretty cool."

NOOOOO! He's missed my entire point. Kate Beckinsale is allowed to be hot *and* a cool person. Most cool people are *super* hot. It's not individual hot people that I'm talking about; it's our dumb-arse culture, which tries to make us believe that the way we look is the most important thing. A culture that says if you look a certain way, then different things will be available to you and you will be treated differently.

But after #hothusband made this remark, I stopped and remembered he was a hot person and just needs to sit there and be pretty, as he doesn't really know what he's talking about, so I patted him on the head and ignored him.

One of my favorite scenes in *30 Rock* (as if there could be only one) was when Tina Fey's character Liz Lemon went out on a date with a hot guy and the waitress was super rude to her and super nice to the hot dude. It was hilarious, because that shit is spot-on. People have always been overly nice to #hothusband and only mediocre to me—until I got internet-famous and started naming and shaming, so now people also throw me some pity attention.

It doesn't stop there, though. #hothusband doesn't know when people are flirting with him. And I don't mean innocent flirting that is acceptable at the school cafeteria; I'm talking full-blown "here's a sneak peek at my nipple" flirting.

We holiday on the Gold Coast a lot. It's near where I grew up, and it's got some totally epic and gnarly surf breaks, so #hothusband is a happy man. And I myself love a happy, hot Maori.

It gets super busy where he surfs, and we always seem to head up there when there is some totally wicked surf competition on, and all the supermodels from Brazil and Japan flock to see the sick surfer dudes do epic shit on waves. OK, no more surfing lingo, it's making me (and no doubt you) nauseous.

So this means the beach is crowded. The beach and the waves are full of people wanting to catch a sweet-arse ride (soz) on a world-famous break. *I* just want to go up and see my family and show the bitches I went to school with what a success I am, but *he's* all about the waves.

The last time we went up, #hothusband got a lot of attention. He usually gets a fair bit, but this time there was extra, because he's a bloody celebrity by osmosis.

He went for a surf, and I frolicked around on the beach with the kids. After he came running in from the surf, *Baywatch*-style, he seemed confused (hot-person confused).

"Are you OK?" I asked.

"Yeah, all good."

I didn't believe him. "What happened?" I pressed.

"Oh, well, I was out there and the surf was awesome and this chick paddled up to me."

I stopped burying my four-year-old in the sand and got up. "Go on," I said without blinking.

"Well, she was just talking to me about the surf . . . ," he started.

"And . . . ?" I questioned, fearing the worst judging by the look on his face.

"That's all. She was just talking to me."

"Right." I relaxed and blinked for what felt like the first time in twenty minutes.

He wasn't as relaxed. "But she was really hot, obviously; she's Brazilian."

"Obviously."

"And she wasn't really wearing anything, and I got confused."

"Confused?"

"Yeah, I didn't know what to do."

"Are you serious?! Because you are both hot and half-naked in the water, you got confused about how to have an adult conversation? Just don't fuck her. It's not hard. She can be sitting on a surfboard talking to you about whatever she wants, and you're allowed to engage, but just because she's hot and you're hot doesn't mean you instantly need to get into each other."

This is what I worry about with the hot ones.

To be completely honest, I don't really care what anyone looks like. That's the whole point—I want the world to be exactly like me when it comes to this issue. Stop valuing people on their appearance and expecting different things from different people judged on the varying degrees of hotness. And I also want Sally Field to be the president of the United States of America. So if someone could get cracking on both those things, I'd really appreciate it.

The One No One Cares About

Times have changed.

Things that used to be common pet peeves, like high-cut swimsuits cutting into places they promised they wouldn't, general nepotism, and people who don't need to wash their hair every day, no longer register on my annoyance radar. What has taken their place is menial shit that shouldn't matter—like rich people filming themselves opening things they were given by other rich people.

This isn't just reserved for us women; it's something that my children are also obsessing over. They are addicted to watching people they will never meet open toys they will never have.

So many things are being given to people who don't need them.

Surely these people don't keep all the things they are given, do they? DO they?! They must regift.

Is this a new thing we are going to start seeing? Influencers regift the gifts they were originally gifted, and then the new person films themselves opening the secondhand gift, and we all watch them and realize that the gift has been regifted, and everyone laughs and cries and no one says "gift" anymore? Is this what Gen Y thinks is charity?

I thought I'd do what any levelheaded adult would do and draft a letter to no one in particular and not send it but instead print it in my book to be read by people it's not intended for.

Dear Influencers,

Sup, fam? I feel like I'm talking to my sorority girlz! Yass, let's celebrate that we are big online and only address each other with the hashtag #girlboss, #queen, or #thisone.

It's fun getting free stuff, isn't it? I know, I get gifted some super-fun things, and it makes me feel so super important and superior. I remember the first month's supply of toilet paper I got. I grabbed that box and ran upstairs screaming for all of my well-dressed children to come and open the gift with me. Every time I had a movement I would wipe with gratitude, and I made sure my children did the same.

It's fun. And it doesn't stop there. I've been sent some pretty fantastic fabric thongs for a dog that I don't have, and I'm still holding on to a vibrator that is anatomically impossible, because I'm not a quitter.

But it's a tricky game, isn't it, my fellow fancy-for-no-real-reason influencing colleagues. Do we receive the gifts and then give a shout-out? Or do we stop looking like arseholes and no longer film ourselves opening gifts from people we will never meet, gifting us things that we and our followers can't afford?

Why do we do this to ourselves, you guys? Why do we torture ourselves into thinking that our followers want to see us indulge our own egos and film ourselves opening stuff?

There are some exceptions, though—I mean, I'm not crazy! Like, if my bank calls me and says they will waive our mortgage or car payment for a month in exchange for me filming myself opening an envelope from them, then I will be filming the shit out of that and there is nothing anyone can do about it, because you're not the boss of me. But lip kits, or $1,400 boots, or those teeny-tiny sunglasses that cost more than that necklace that old lady on the *Titanic* wore, people don't need to see me opening this shit. We are smug enough as it is, running around getting free accommodations and invited to fancy lunches, all because we're big online.

Let's all make a pact right here and vow that we will stop filming ourselves opening gifts on Instagram, or if we have to because we are contracted to and it's our only talent, let's all pinkie-swear to be better at it. Let's have a few #sponsored wines and pretend to be shocked and surprised about a gift that we have made our manager and agent hustle for for six months.

And while we're on the subject, why are we getting these gifts anyway? I mean, we already have everything we need and everything that anyone wants: followers #blessed. I really think companies need to be throwing the free stuff around to people who need it, the forgotten brothers and sisters of the world, the ones who work really hard and get no credit, like Rob Kardashian or that Hilton brother.

Anyway, babes, so good to chat. Looking forward to seeing y'all at the next event where our faces are the same and we only look at each other through a screen that our dads pay the bill for.

Best,

C x

The One Where I Became an Anti-Influencer

It seems that anyone can get paid to do anything these days. And I mean *anything*.

Gone are the days when I was a kid and adults I knew would have three jobs, working as a part-time schoolteacher, weekend vet, and every other day a dental hygienist. These days you can pick some lint from your belly button, blog about it, and all of a sudden you've got an office and three staff members working for you because you're the highest-paid "belly dissection guru" in the country.

There's a character on *The Real Housewives of Beverly Hills* who is an accountability coach—yep, she gets paid to text "clients" to make sure they have done their daily workout or drunk enough water. She also claims to be the most real and down to earth of the housewives, something that Erika Jayne and I have a few things to say about.

But it's still a formula, one that I'm happy and feel obliged to break down for you.

Step One: Be attractive.

Step Two: Open a bank account.

Step Three: Find different ways to hold things.

Step Four: Get a degree in Photoshop.

Step Five: Deposit money into newly opened bank account.

Step Six: Repeat.

I have posted around nine hundred #celestechallengeaccepted photos and been paid for fifteen. I'm not good at doing things that don't feel right. I have the same approach to anal sex; it doesn't feel right, so I don't do it.

I get approached by a lot of companies to promote their products. The main ones are detox tea, meal replacements, and diet pills, and I'm not interested. I'm not interested at all. I always respond with the same comment:

"I don't promote any products that make women think they need to look a certain way to feel a certain way."

Then I dance around the house naked to "Run the World" and feel like I've really done something good for humanity.

The thing is, Instagram success seems to have a certain reputation to it. Insta models, influencers, they are all things that I'm not. I'm an actor and a comedian. I am so super grateful for this platform, but that's how I see it: as a platform for my work, not as my profession.

I've started hearing a lot of things about my "brand." "Did you say no to that because it's not in keeping with your brand?" Brand? What? No. I just think trying to sell weight-loss tablets to new mums is bullshit, and I don't want to do it. Never mind selling out and ruining my "brand"; it's just a mean thing to make women feel they need to look any different to be better at life.

The internet can be a bit of a bitch at times. Not a fun Chelsea Handler type of bitch who encourages us women to support each other and keeps us accountable for our actions. It's more of a Khloe Kardashian calling her mum Kris a whore type of bitch.

The internet has the ability to make us feel nice about ourselves, but it seems it has more of a tendency to make us question how we parent or whether our above-knee area should be better defined.

It has made the world a smaller place, to the extent that we know stuff that's going on on the other side of the world instantly. Just the other day I heard that the queen was at Fashion Week. I mean, shit, you guys, if that isn't revolutionary, I don't know what is.

But at the moment, Pornhub has greater success at making us feel good than bloggers do. I love that the internet has brought us closer and made doctors out of strippers. But it also allows haters to hate and feel as though we should all give a shit about what we are all saying at all times.

I'm not a blogger—not a mommy blogger, a fashion blogger, not even a food blogger (although I think if I had to pick one, this would be the type of blogging I could really put my back into). I'm not a columnist, I don't tweet a lot, and I try to steer clear of anything that associates me with anything other than being an actor, comedian, and writer.

I have met a few bloggers—oh my God, do they have thick skin. "It's part of the job," they say. "I need to look over comments and listen to my audience." They take on advice, then construct an articulate response that either takes into account all of what everyone is saying or polarizes everyone, thus gaining them more traction; then the cycle starts again and regains momentum.

No thank you, I'm not at all interested in this world. I create content with the purpose of making people laugh and to maybe show how ridiculous the culture of celebrity and fame is. I'm happy that what I do sometimes starts conversations, but I don't then scroll through the comments and respond to what people say or suggest.

When I first started getting attention for my craft (Can you call taking your clothes off and taking funny photos of yourself all in the name of comedy a craft? Well, if Paris Hilton can plug her iPod into a speaker in Ibiza and call herself a DJ, then what I do is a craft, goddamn it!), I would read all the comments. All of them. It would be a family affair. The stepdaughters would scream out, "OMG, Sarah Hyland just started following you!" or "Paris Hilton just liked one of your photos" or "You're not my real mum! I hate you!"

Api started to take on a security-guard role. While we were lying in bed on our phones (romance ain't dead in my house, girlzzz), he would mutter without taking his eyes off his screen, "Username Nutface255 commented, he wants to tap your fat arse; you should block him." Or "Username Peacedream is really sweet and she wants to know where you got your dress from; you should let her know via a private message, babe, and maybe let her know how many colors it comes in." My husband doesn't do things by halves.

Those were the early days, but now I've got a different attitude. I don't read, and I don't respond.

If people want to look at my photos and call me fat, I mean I don't love it, but I'll get through it. If people look at what I do and decide to call the people I'm parodying dumb, skinny bitches, they are TOTALLY missing the point, but I'm not their mum—they can self-regulate, and if living in a basement and being mean to people is how you go about your day, who am I to judge?

I'm not here to tell anyone what they should think about what I do. I'm just showing you another side, a real side, hopefully the funny side. This is why I wouldn't make a good blogger; I'm not great at interaction, and I don't have the tools or energy to defend what I do, to explain what I do. I'm all about the doing and not the talking about the doing. As Amy Poehler says, "The talking about the thing isn't the thing. The doing of the thing is the thing." I don't want to talk about it—I want to keep doing it.

So often I have people say to me, "You should use your platform to do THIS or THIS," and I think, "Yep, you're totally right, I should use my platform to bring attention to the inhumane treatment of sloths in captivity, but that's not why I started this. I started this to make people laugh, and because I was pretty sick of feeling shit about myself for not feeling the way social media was telling me I needed to feel."

But then one day I decided to get a bit crazy.

I decided to engage, and fuck me, didn't it backfire. I did something nice, and the internet got mad. Really mad.

I met this lady—let's call her Charitable McCharity Face—through a charity we are both ambassadors for. McCharity Face is a blogger and "shot to fame" over years and years of writing and blogging. She wrote a hilarious post that resonated with people around the world about what it's like to have sex with your husband in between spending time with your kids; then some online news websites got onto her and the rest is hard work and history. She also did some reality TV when she was younger, but we are all dickheads and do stupid stuff in our twenties. She's really transparent with her community, and she looks after them as much as they look after her, it seems.

On this particular day she was having a rough time at home with her now ex-husband, and she posted a photo of herself bawling on the floor of a hotel bathroom. This is her thing—she's so open and honest that she allows us to see her, warts and all. She looked sad. Really sad.

I get sadness. I'm sure there are a lot of us who do. It's a bloody horrible, isolating place that is dark and cold. And on this day she seemed consumed by darkness and needed everyone she usually supports to know just how sad she was.

This isn't something that I do, but I totally understand why she and others do it. They set up a space, a community that's safe and supportive, so when things happen to them personally they feel supported and safe within their village. I feel just as loved by my followers, but I think I have more of an audience than a village or community; I guess that's the actor in me. Different strokes for different internet folks.

McCharity Face is strong, seemingly fearless, brash, loud, honest, flawed, vulnerable, and above all real. Really bloody real, and now that she is in the public eye because of her realness, everyone wants a piece of her, and they will take whatever they can get, no matter the cost.

Her community is full of misfit queens, and she has created a space where we are all OK with not being OK. So on this dark day I called on that community, *her* community, to help her out.

A nice lady from McCharity Face's community had contacted me, letting me know she had set up a GoFundMe account for McCharity Face if people wanted to throw in a few dollars so our friend could grab a bottle of wine or take herself away from the world that so frequently embraces or attacks her. Not a big deal, just what mates do. It was also a way for people to kind of give back to her, as she has been inundated with confessions from so many women that she singlehandedly talked them "off the ledge."

As I'm the self-proclaimed Beyoncé of the internet and thought I could get more reach, I did an impromptu Livestream letting people know what was going on and telling them if they wanted to be involved, then they could.

Well, didn't I prove to be a silly little internet Beyoncé.

The abuse came thick and fast. It wasn't the abuse of the traditional troll; there wasn't any "you're a dumb bitch—I'm going to cut your toes off." It was much more sophisticated. They went straight to the heart. "My niece has a rare heart condition. You should be helping her, not getting money to buy someone wine." Ouch.

There were so many super-nice people who just jumped on board and either threw a few bucks at the campaign or left a nice "great idea" message. There were also people who did nothing; I like them just as much. Then there were the people who thought being rude and hurtful would get them their desired outcome.

You know what they say about opinions.

When McCharity Face saw what was going on, she begged me to shut it all down. This pissed me off. I had wanted to help out, and I know there was a huge number of people who wanted to do something as well. That's the beginning, middle, and end of it. I was so annoyed that people then saw this as an opportunity to tell me who I can and can't support. They had gone to the zoo and poked the bear, so I got all Bethenny Frankel on the internet.

McCharity Face is incredible. She responds to people who write to her, gives crazy shout-outs, and is generally connected to her community. She makes me look as though I'm the forgotten middle redheaded cousin when it comes to raising funds. I know ambassadorship isn't a competition. I'm not completely sure "ambassadorship" is even a word, but if it is, then she's beating the tits off me. I know she and the charity don't see it like this, but that's because she's winning. No winner sees anything as competition; it takes a loser to bring that to their attention.

I closed the campaign, and McCharity Face and I decided to donate the money raised to Rafiki Mwema, a charity helping sexually abused children in Kenya that we are both quite heavily involved in. I did another Livestream and advised that the money was now going to a charity.

People still weren't happy, and unlike my fellow Rafiki ambassador, I didn't care. I was over it.

Ellen DeGeneres (Does she even need her last name? Would y'all know who I was talking about if I just wrote Ellen? DM me.) says that you should read the bad comments as well as the good. You can't just take in the good.

This is one thing I don't agree with when it comes to Ellen DeG— oh, you know who I mean. I don't take the good with the bad at all. I'm the boss of what I read, so if I want to read only the good, then I will. I have A LOT of honest people around me who are more than happy to jump at the opportunity to tell me when I'm shit, so I'm happy for my audience to blow smoke up my ass in the knowledge that the people closest to me—my inner circle, my lifeline—will be right by my side with a fire extinguisher to shut that shit down if it looks as though it's getting out of hand.

No matter what you do, there will always be people who don't like it. I'm sure these are the same people who complain about the afternoon sun on a winter's day being too bright or kids having too much fun at a park.

I wish I could end this chapter with some amazing InstaQuote about rising above the haters, but I hate uninvited advice—both giving and taking it. I just think if it doesn't involve you, don't get involved.

The Last One Part 1
(Celisticles)

Twelve unknown facts about me that I'm sure you are all dying to know:

1. Eight is my favorite number.
2. #hothusband is nine years older than me.
3. I was born and raised in Porpoise Spit (google *Muriel's Wedding* for reference).
4. In my sister's speech at my wedding, we both cried over the fake dead brother we never had.
5. I did three years of full-time singing lessons, and I still am pitchy AF.
6. I danced as a cheerleader in two National Rugby League grand finals; Tina Turner performed the halftime entertainment and was amazing, and the Broncos girls were the bitchiest.
7. I couldn't care less about *Game of Thrones*.
8. *Friends* is the greatest show in the whole wide world, and if you don't agree with me, you are the dumbest of all the dum-dums.

9. I can't read hashtags; I hate hashtags—all those words and letters squashed together into one long, dumb-sounding word are confusing.
10. My cat's breath smells like cat food.
11. I never really got into *Seinfeld*.
12. When I was eight my religion teacher told me if I couldn't look at the sun for five minutes without blinking, I didn't love Jesus.

Four things that have been said to me as a female comedian:

1. "You might be more successful if your content wasn't so much 'about the ladies.'"
2. "Hey, I really like the jeans you wore during your set."
3. "You should get a guy to open for you—you might sell more tickets."
4. "You look great with your hair up."

Five things you can only say to people who are "your" people:

1. "I'd trade two of my other friends to spend more time with you."
2. "I'll come over, but I don't want to talk. Can we just stare at the TV in the same room together?"
3. "Can I borrow some undies?"
4. "As soon as my husband dies, we are on!"
5. "Your mum needs to cut her hair."

Six unofficial nicknames I've been called:

1. Lip-Neck (as I have no chin, and I go straight from my lip to my neck)
2. Fat Ricki Lee
3. Gillette, "the Best a Man Can Get"
4. Elephant (there is a character named Celeste in the *Babar* cartoon books)
5. Phyllis (this is what everyone I speak to on the phone thinks my name is)
6. Moleste (because it rhymes with Celeste, not because I was a super-horny teenager and was up for a dry hump any day of the week [awkward smile emoji])

Four things that blow my mind:

1. How Chris Brown is not in jail
2. Cate Blanchett's skin
3. How Botox really works and doesn't kill people
4. People who can surf

Ten things I've learned about my body:

1. I've got a lot of gas. In a good way.
2. My wrists are really thin.
3. My legs are my thing.
4. I dislocated my hips when giving birth both times. If I sit down for too long, it takes my left hip a while to click back in, and I hobble around as though I have hemorrhoids that are playing up. Which I'm proud to say I don't.

5. My chest is covered in scars and is numb at times.
6. I have a long bum. It goes down to the back of my knees.
7. I have my nana's feet.
8. My hair is limp, limp hair.
9. My breasts are closer to my belly button than my chin.
10. I'm rather flexible.

Five things I've been told about my face and body:

1. I have fat pockets where a jawline should be.
2. I have drag-queen eyelids. This is always given as a compliment, and taken as one.
3. I look like a bird.
4. I have a face that people don't like—not an ugly face, not a bad face, just a face that people don't like.
5. I don't have earlobes. I watched Kris Jenner in an episode of *Keeping Up with the Kardashians* (I know I could have written *KUWTK* and everyone would have known what I was talking about, but I've got a word count to hit, you guys), and she was completely freaked out by her earlobes. She's had reconstructive surgery on her earlobes. Just another thing that we need to fucking freak out about. Our earlobes.

The Last One Part 2 (Acknowledgments)

Big fat thank-you to:

Mum and Dad for all of it. Liv for making all of it fun.

Benny, Harry, Angus, and Violet for being the loudest cheer squad a gal could ask for.

Catherine Milne for being the kindest publisher a dyslexic first-time author could ask for.

Shannon Kelly and Emma Dowden for making me sound really smart.

Sahra for the cups of tea and excitement at any news I deliver. And the cookies, oh the cookies.

Kyah for reminding me I'm not as great as I sometimes want to think I am.

Thomas for being the greatest witch ever.

Kika for letting me call at all times crying, saying "I can't do it," and making everything OK.

Weez and Brookie for Wednesday night family dinners, which were dominated by me talking about this book.

Lisa for thinking I'm fancy and saying so.

Api for giving me Lou and Buddy, everything that is important to me.

Meryl Streep. For obvious reasons.

Dear Parents

If you cry in the liquor store, you'll almost always get a discount on wine.
    C x

About the Author

Celeste (actor, writer, comedian) has put all the words she has ever learned into this book, yet her publishers still want an author bio (exhausted face emoji). (I wrote a whole book on who I am and you can basically see my whole life on Instagram! What more do you people want from me?!) As a starting point, Celeste is happily married (sorry, fellas), a mum to two cute and full-on boys, an evil stepmum to two teenaged girls, and is more of a dog person—she never really understood the whole cat thing.